Ice Cream
the delicious history

MARILYN POWELL

THE OVERLOOK PRESS
Woodstock & New York

First published in the United States in 2006 by
The Overlook Press, Peter Mayer Publishers, Inc.
Woodstock and New York

NEW YORK:
141 Wooster Street
New York, NY 10012

WOODSTOCK:
One Overlook Drive
Woodstock, NY 12498
www.overlookpress.com
[for individual orders, bulk and special sales, contact our Woodstock office]

∞ The paper used in this book meets the requirements for paper
permanence as described in the ANSI Z39.48-1992 standard.

Cataloging-in-Publication Data is available from the Library of Congress

Manufactured in the United States of America
FIRST EDITION
ISBN 1-58567-797-3
1 3 5 7 9 10 8 6 4 2

For my sister, Gwyneth Mary,
whom I know and love simply as Gwyn

CONTENTS

INTRODUCTION

SO YOU WANT TO KNOW ABOUT ICE CREAM

You're already familiar with its taste—cold and sweet; its texture—smooth; its body—firm. And you wait for ice cream to be soft enough to scoop, so you understand what its nature requires. But you want to know more.

Okay, here are some facts. The ice-cream dipper or scoop was invented in the nineteenth century. In 1925, a scoop that was heart-shaped was designed, making it possible for chocolate and vanilla hearts to kiss, side by side, in a bowl. In the 1930s, a scoop with defrosting fluid in the handle appeared and soon became the industry standard. Interested?

Well, no, you say, you want more than facts. You had in mind a *history* of ice cream.

All right, I promise you this book will deal with the history. However, I should tell you at the outset, it's not a straightforward account. There's the history of ice cream—which is whatever is known about its past, including the proliferation into kinds (ice milk, granita, sherbet, gelato) and into sorts (soda, sundae, cone)—and there's the romance of ice cream. And the two overlap. At least one tall tale ascribes the origin of ice cream to accident—sweet cream left outside in the freezing cold, that sort of thing—as though the stuff were too curious, too potent, to be left to mere human engineering. And accident becomes a narrative element. Much that happens to ice cream seems to happen by chance. Sodas were discovered that way; so were sundaes, according to the tale-tellers. Now you understand why this book is more than a textbook history of ice cream. It recounts the facts and sometimes ventures into myth. It's organized by themes, not chronology. That strikes me as appropriate to the subject itself, the consummate shape-shifter, flowing from one form into another, from liquid to solid and back into liquid again.

Ice cream is unusual in many ways. Perhaps because it's eaten frozen in winter as well as summer, perhaps because it appears to defy the seasons and even, in a way, common sense, it has been invested with special properties over the centuries. It's been enlisted to meet a surprising range of human desires.

A while ago, I was looking at ice-cream statistics. I'm not referring to those that report on how many containers were produced or consumed in any given year—not those routine industry statistics. I'm talking about the ones that appear in the *Guinness Book of World Records*. For instance, the largest banana split in the world was made by the employees of Palm Dairies, in Edmonton, Alberta, in 1988. The split consisted of 44,689 pounds of ice cream, 9,688 pounds of chocolate syrup, and 537 pounds of toppings. It stretched four and a half miles, for heaven's sake. As for the world's largest ice-cream bar, it was produced by Augusto Ltd., in Kalisz, Poland, in 1994, and weighed an outrageous 19,357 pounds. The world's largest milkshake (a classic black and white, by the way, chocolate and vanilla ice cream) was mixed by the Comfort Diner in New York City in 2000 and amounted to a whopping 6,000 gallons. Mercy, that's the equivalent of 50,000 individual, normal-sized, shakes!

There I go with the facts again! But they do point out that ice cream is not just a food. In this case, it's been publicity stunt and communal sport. Everyone climbed kitchen stepladders to reach the top of the ice-cream monuments. Everyone enjoyed seeing and ultimately eating them. Moreover, by the time you read about the

There is one recipe I want to single out here: Mrs. Hannah Glasse's eighteenth-century recipe for raspberry cream ice. Not that it's particularly praiseworthy. Rather, it's representative, and its author was very influential. Let's just say I want to plead the distaff side in the ice-cream chronicles because there are enough male chefs who are known and celebrated for their ice-cream artistry. Mrs. Glasse preferred to be called "a good English Cook." She is mentioned briefly in this book, but let me enlarge on her biography here. She was the author of *The Art of Cookery, Made Plain and Easy*, published in 1747, and *The Compleat Confectioner* (about a decade later), in which she remarked that ice cream was "a thing us'd in all deserts," quite a fad at the best dinners in London. When Mrs. Hannah Glasse died in 1770, ice cream had taken hold. This is her recipe, as it appeared in the 1751 edition of *The Art of Cookery*:

Take two Pewter Basons, one larger than the other; the inward one must have a close Cover, into which you are to put your Cream, and mix it with Raspberries or whatever you like best, to give it a Flavour and a Colour. Sweeten it to your Palate; then cover it close, and set it into the larger Bason. Fill it with Ice and a Handful of Salt; let it stand in this Ice three Quarters of an Hour, then uncover it, and stir the Cream well together; cover it close again and let it stand Half an Hour longer, after that turn it to your Plate.

If there were only one stirring before serving, the result on the plate must have been unevenly frozen and icy. But popularize the recipe Mrs. Hannah Glasse did. Her *Art of Cookery* went through about seventeen editions by the time the century was over. Even Martha Washington owned a copy.

How times have changed. Published in 1995, Caroline Liddell and Robin Weir's *Frozen Desserts: The Definitive Guide to Making Ice Creams, Ices, Sorbets, Gelati, and Other Frozen Delights* contains pages and pages of recipes that would cause Mrs. Glasse to flush with envy. (In fact, it's one of their recipes, the Ultimate Chocolate Ice Cream, that my friend Michèle is following in chapter 3 of this book. Just don't confuse it with Mrs. Marshall's recipe for an equally extravagant chocolate ice reprinted in the same chapter.) But *Frozen Desserts* is also a little miscellany of ice-cream history, and it includes a cartoon from the authors' collection that I particularly like.

Here's the situation. A lady and gentleman, c. 1830, are sitting in an English ice-cream parlour, eating and discussing their "frozen delight." The lady complains that ice cream is too cold. The gentleman responds by recommending that the chill be removed in the future. Ice cream was such a novelty then. What a long way it's come, baby.

According to *The New York Times Magazine* of October 31, 2004, salesmen for David Michael & Co. travel their territory in the United States selling manufactured flavours for a variety of foods, among them ice cream. More than a hundred companies across the country compete to sell their wares. More than a thousand vanillas are available from one company alone. There's a difference between a strawberry that tastes fresh or cooked, is "floral" or "meaty." Bench tests are done to determine whether bubble gum or cotton candy flavours are approved. Food scientists concoct and rule.

The process seems too clinical for ice cream, doesn't it? I confess I'm drawn to personal anecdote, gathered from the dead and the living. As you'll discover, friends and family have been plagued by my questions for this book. There's testimony as well from others whom I discovered along the way and persuaded to talk about ice cream. In other words, emphasis is placed on personal communication.

A couple of years ago, I paid a visit to the Bilboquet ice-cream parlour on rue Bernard in Montreal. It was an early-spring afternoon; the sun was shining, and the sidewalk was crowded with customers. Many were lined up right to the front door to buy ice cream, and many others, including my friend and me, were sitting at the outdoor tables. A strong breeze was blowing. It was too soon to be outside eating ice cream, really, but the warm sun seemed to remind everyone of lazy, hazy days to come. "Try the maple," my friend said. A Quebec specialty, $6.00 a dish, the most expensive item on the menu, it arrived with a little cookie in the shape of a maple leaf on the side of the dish. By the end of April, the flowing and gathering of sap, as well as the boiling of syrup, had just finished. The ice cream was studded with candy—called taffy—that is made by throwing hot maple syrup onto the snow. The syrup solidifies, forming sweet, hard, polished crystals. No food scientist manufactured these crystals. In my mouth, the ice cream pooled around taffy that deliciously, slowly, dissolved on my tongue.

At the next table, two small children were squirming, waiting for their mother to return from inside the parlour. At last she emerged, pushed her way through the long line condensed milk and "still freeze" it (no churning, little stirring) in the manner of Mrs. Hannah Glasse. My older brother, John, brought home store-bought ice cream. He had a Saturday job, and he'd spend some of his pay on treats for my sister and me. As soon as he'd open the door, he'd call out, "Boola!"—a code name for tuck that, as best as he can recall, he found in his reading of boys' books. My sister and I would race up the stairs behind him, straight to his room, where he'd dish out ice cream for the three of us. My mother and father weren't privy to what was happening, and the conspiracy made the feast all the more delectable. When I turned eighteen, friends took me out for dinner at an ice-cream parlour, that remarkable public space devoted to the enthusiastic consumption of the sweet. I couldn't have chosen a better place to celebrate. My love for ice cream has been constant.

Originally, I imagined this book as an elaboration of a documentary I produced in 2001 for CBC Radio's *Ideas*. It was an affectionate send-up of the intellectualism of the program for which I worked, a kind of "the joke's on us" undertaking. On the radio, I applied John Stuart Mill's theory of the pleasure principle to the enjoyment of ice cream. I was being facetious, and he would not have approved. I'd intended to substitute ice cream for cocaine—as in Freud's enthusiasm for the latter—and play with the idea of obsession, but reconsidered in the end. There were limits to facetiousness. When I set out to write a book on ice cream, however, I chose a different path, one that I believed was more conventional, more "authorly." I would be more serious.

Then, in the middle of my research, I began to grow anxious about large gaps in information that existed. Ice cream seemed to jump out of myth in the distant past into a very European history in the seventeenth and eighteenth centuries. No wonder Elizabeth David spent so many of the last years of her life delving through old travel narratives and cookbooks, searching for references that would help to illuminate and explain. Anyone familiar with David's extraordinary posthumous work, *The Harvest of the Cold Months: The Social History of Ice and Ices,* will be aware that I'm tremendously indebted to her research and insights. Even so, I reckon someone else will come along with new evidence, retrieved from some dusty old travel account that's lain undisturbed on a shelf somewhere for ages—and completely change everyone's assumptions. Until that happens, I have to admit to gaps I haven't been able to fill. But I've been freed to concentrate on patterns of meaning, ideas of ice cream—I guess you could say the original premise of the radio documentary has proved its worth, after all (and I'm not being facetious). Or perhaps it was the splendid example of Margaret Visser in her book *Much Depends on Dinner* that influenced me. At any rate, I'm not presenting you with a study; it's not exhaustive; it's my take on ice cream. You have yours too, I'm sure.

This is how I like to picture you out there. You're holding the book in one hand and a spoon in the other. You pause from reading to dip the spoon into the bowl of ice cream in front of you, then back to the text. And so it goes, back and forth. Because, as far as I'm concerned, the book should never stray far from the primary act of eating ice cream. But I hope that reading it takes you deep into your own life experiences. You have your own tales to tell and your own family history.

If you eat ice cream, you're in pursuit of a pleasure that began with a shock: your initiation into surprisingly cold and transitory bliss. A falling cone gave you an appreciation of comedy and tragedy, how quickly one turns into the other. And yet you continue to pursue ice cream because you've never outgrown the bliss. Ice cream's been the sweet of choice at a birthday party, the treat at a sickbed, a confection at weddings. You encounter it again and again.

You don't eat ice cream to satisfy physical hunger. If food were labelled "essential" or "frivolous," ice cream obviously would belong in the "frivolous" category. Manna in the Bible, after all, was probably insect waste and a matter of survival. On the other hand, it's easy to imagine that the ambrosia enjoyed by the gods on Mount Olympus (not the version your grandmother used to make with miniature marshmallows) was some sort of ice cream that could grant immortality. At the very least, the presence of ice cream in your life makes you happy. That puts you in the company of, among others, Louis XIV, Franklin Delano Roosevelt, and Giuseppe Tomasi di Lampedusa, who, in his marvellous novel *Il Gattopardo (The Leopard),* sets out ices on the teeming board at a Palermo ball—pink, champagne, and coffee, elegant parfaits, Lampedusa notes, that fall apart with a squelch as the knife pierces their depths. There's even "hot ice cream for cold days" behind a closed door in Roald Dahl's *Charlie and the Chocolate Factory.*

The point is, this book rests on the premise that reading about ice cream affords its own kind of pleasure, parallel to the indulgence of eating it. References from literature and art are on an equal footing with recorded fact. The distant past is pretty much conjecture, as I've explained, and the more recent past, shaped largely by commercial ice-cream makers and sellers, contains its own share of make-believe. So the story's all of a piece. Fiction complements, colours, inflates, distorts, and enhances reality, creating a confection of its own. This book is about ice cream and its kin (ice milk, granita, sherbet, gelato) and also about the culture of ice cream. I promise you won't have any difficulty telling the real from the imaginary.

1

A TASTE FOR COLD

Ah, nostalgia! In a world gone by—well, not so long ago—a little ritual used to take place on hot summer days. Perhaps you're old enough to remember, or your parents or grandparents told you about it. When ice was carried by horse and wagon and then by truck, children were drawn to it irresistibly. They'd watch and wait for the iceman to split off a block with his pick and carry it up the walk to make a home delivery. And, when the coast was clear, they'd snatch up the shards that were left behind. They sucked or crunched them, biting down on them with their teeth. The ice squeaked and shattered, filling their cheeks with silvery fragments, good for cooling off. That scene at the back of the wagon or truck was all about a taste for cold, and it wasn't new.

Putting ice in the mouth is an old, old practice. The ancient Greeks and Romans added crushed ice to their wine to cool it and, therefore, themselves. Perhaps, delicately, politely, they let the ice melt to a liquid on their tongue, without crushing it with their teeth. As for the Arabs of the distant past, they were masters of a drink they called *sharab*. That's what the word means in classical Arabic: "a drink." It was concocted from a luscious array of possibilities—orange, lemon, quince, cranberry, cherry, apricot, plum, grape, or pomegranate syrup, spices and blossoms—mixed with water, to which were added ice or snow. But the word began to be used for a drink that contained alcohol as well, and so, in the late Middle Ages, a new word was coined, *sharbat,* from which our word *sherbet* is derived.

You see where this is going. From ice to ... if not full-bodied dairy ice cream, then possibly granita, a host of smallish ice crystals suspended in a frozen concoction of water, sugar, and flavouring. Yum. The texture is coarse, the ice crystals detectable, as they're not supposed to be in ice cream.

But wait a minute, I hear you saying, granita is Sicilian, not Arabian. Well, Sicily was colonized by the Greeks and Romans, and in the ninth and tenth centuries was under Arab rule. The Sicilians are supposed to have learned how to make granita and sherbet from the Arabs, who are supposed to have discovered how to freeze their *sharab,* later *sharbat.* And where do you suppose the Arabs got the idea?

As writer Annie Dillard says in her book *The Writing Life,* "To find a honey tree, first catch a bee." And then she describes a process of releasing the captured bee, observing where it goes, capturing another and doing the same, letting the bees lead your search until you see them enter the tree. Dillard credits Henry David Thoreau with alerting her to this watchful pursuit of honey, which she uses as an approach to writing and I'm using to trace ice cream as far back as I can. Of course, I'm beginning with a bee that's not a bee at all but an iceman. After all, to understand a taste for cold, it makes sense to keep an eye on him. Ice travels. Not simply in floes but culturally, socially, and it has a documented history.

What follows, then, is a leap back into a time within reach, with connections that reach back earlier still. It's unlikely a culture will be found that munched its way happily through ice, as some people, these days, champ down on ice cubes. But one thing is certain: there was a natural progression from ice to ice cream.

Spadina House sits on a hill with a view that once looked down, unobstructed, all the way to Lake Ontario. Today, it's a museum on a circular drive that feeds onto a street in Toronto, the city in which I live. Complete with original furniture, paintings, and art objects, the house is witness to the tastes of successive generations of two families, Victorian and Edwardian. Everything is as it was, as though they were still in residence.

Spadina House still has the icebox—or "refrigerator," as it was known then—that the family purchased in 1909. I make an appointment with Fiona Lucas to see the relic. She works as a program officer at the house and she has written a paper about the icebox.

"The refrigerator could hold about 600 pounds of ice," she says. I'm impressed. The average home model held anywhere from 50 to 125 pounds. "It was probably designed for commercial use," Lucas explains. Its sheer size—four and a half feet wide, seven feet deep, and fifteen feet high—made it necessary for a room to be built behind the kitchen to accommodate it. A grown man could lie down in its upper ice compartment. "There's a door high up on the wall for the ice to come through—see it?" Fiona Lucas gestures towards the back of the ice compartment. "And there's the remnants of a pulley system. The iceman would bring his wagon up the drive to the small, square service door. The ice would be pulleyed up and pushed through the door." All this choreography was possible because the icebox sits against an exterior wall of the house.

The Eureka, to give it its company name, was top of the line. There's a locker at the rear, for hanging meat, which would have been insulated with sawdust. At the front are four compartments lined with opal enamel, which wouldn't chip, was a non-conductor, and resistant to moisture. Its doors are oak. Naturally, the Eureka did its daily job of keeping food fresh. But it represented so much more.

At the moment it was purchased, it was the latest in ice-house architecture that already stretched over millennia. There is evidence of ice pits in Iron Age Britain and records of ice houses in Mesopotamia almost four thousand years ago. Alexander the Great ordered snow pits dug and layered with oak branches when he set out to conquer the city of Petra in 837 BC. Ice was stored in pits, caves, wells, and cellars. Materials for construction varied—mud, brick, stone, wood. And insulation was provided by sand, ash, straw, sawdust, sheepskin, even goat hair and rabbit fur. The Persians covered their underground chambers with conical stacks or hillocks that resembled giant beehives, some of which rose seventy feet above ground.

As for Europe, in the sixteenth century, the king of Denmark ordered a thatched-roof ice house built on his estate at Elsinore—precisely the place to keep the "funeral bak'd meats" that, as Hamlet puts it, "coldly furnish forth the marriage tables" of his mother and uncle. Except there's little evidence of that kind of practice until a couple of centuries later. In the eighteenth century, shelves for food *were* being installed in English ice houses. Yet by then, the Chinese had been refrigerating fish and fruit for thousands of years.

Kings and conquerors had their ice houses. Emperors, khans, and presidents had theirs. And just plain estate owners followed suit. Before the arrival of the icebox at Spadina, an ice house once stood on the grounds, but obviously it was much more convenient to locate that kind of structure indoors. Enter the Eureka, along with the iceman to supply it.

"We still have bills from the 1930s for ice delivery," Fiona Lucas tells me, "and I was looking this morning at the bill for August 1934, when 113 hundred-pound blocks were delivered." (Blocks were available in different weights.) "So that's about five and a half tons of ice. It must have been a hot month." What were they doing with all that ice? Making ice cream, for one thing. At the very least, keeping it frozen until it was served. By then, an ice-cream culture had developed, as events in the history of Spadina House make clear.

At the beginning of the twentieth century, Albert Austin, a prosperous businessman, was the house's owner. His wife, Mary, liked to entertain on a grand scale, with teas, dances, dinner parties, fêtes, and garden parties, and she could afford to hire professionals. A receipt survives in Spadina's archives from the Harry Webb Co., Caterers, Bakers and Manufacturing Confectioners, for a garden party in June 1900 attended by some 310 guests. In addition to the sandwiches and watercress rolls, punch, cakes, and fresh fruit, Mary ordered three gallons of Neapolitan ice cream (the kind in layers, introduced to the rest of the world by makers from Naples in the nineteenth century) and three gallons of strawberry ice cream. To be on the safe side, as a note in her own hand attests, she then ordered more punch and a gallon of vanilla ice cream, and half a gallon of orange water ice.

The frozen fare was to be set out on "ice plates" (also provided by the caterer). Dating back at least to Madame de Pompadour, who, on another June day in 1754, commissioned "plateaux" in white and gold china, ice cream has had dishes, goblets, cups, bowls, glasses, and eventually cutlery—spoons and forks manufactured by Tiffany's, no less—devoted to it. In short, in the circles in which Mary and Albert Austin moved, ice cream involved expensive equipment and ingredients and required special handling. Especially on a warm June day.

In her 1885 *Book of Ices,* Mrs. A. B. Marshall of London recommended that presentation at any social gathering should be fastidiously planned:

At large parties two sorts of ices are usually served, and should be carefully contrasted. A pleasing variety is often produced by filling little moulds with different kinds of ice, which are then served in tiny lace paper cups, under the name *glaces assorties* ... Another very popular form is the Neapolitan ice.

Mary Austin was right in fashion. Mrs. Marshall also advised the use of a Neapolitan box to achieve the layers, a box she manufactured, of course. Though it could be any of two or more flavours, in North America, Neapolitan was usually vanilla, chocolate, and strawberry layers. And so it has remained.

(By the way, in English, "ice"—with or without milk, cream, or eggs—has proved an umbrella term for a dessert that has journeyed through centuries, covered a vast terri-

8

they were served, the ices would have been kept in the equivalent of Mrs. Marshall's "ice cave" (a long, narrow portable metal box lined with ice, which she advertised for use "during Balls, Evening and Garden Parties") or stored in something larger—the ice house, and, in time, the icebox.

Yes, I'm embellishing. The context, however, is fact. Without the iceman, who hefted blocks of ice weighing twenty-five, fifty, or a hundred pounds and delivered them to the property, there would have been no ice cream to remember. Between dances, the ladies and gentlemen would have perspired. Gentility would have suffered from the lack of cold, restorative refreshment. Unthinkable.

By the 1930s, the iceman, with his pick, hook, and tongs, was a familiar visitor to Spadina House—just as electric refrigerators were taking over the market and beginning to put an end to his business for good. Eventually, along would come electric freezers, giving ice cream a longer shelf life, and the direct connection to the past would be broken. So, picture the Austins, on the lawn of their house, enjoying the view down to the city and the lake in the distance. They're indulging in peach sherbet. It's a delicate, elegiac moment; rosy signs of twilight are in the sky. Each spoonful settles in the mouth, half solid, half liquid, gently melting away—a reminder of the transitory nature of life and of pleasure. This is the essence of ice cream, but never so intensely experienced as in the age of the iceman. No wonder a mythology grew up around it.

The practice is ancient. Everywhere the summer was intense, everywhere there were mountains—from the Taurus range in Turkey to the Himalayas in India and the Atlas mountains in North Africa—men went up into them to collect ice and snow. There's even this reference in the Bible: "As the cold of snow in the time of harvest, so is a faithful messenger to them that send him" (Proverbs 25:13). Snow was so valued, it was "harvested" as a crop, in other words. Under the Ottoman rulers of the Turkish Empire, the Moghuls of Northern India, in the lands of the Persians and, of course, the Arabs, a harvest of ice and snow was packed, stacked, and even sold in the marketplace. The Greeks, who probably adopted the habit of cooling their drinks and building ice houses from Middle Easterners, used to climb Mount Olympus to gather snow they sold in the market as early as the fifth century BC.

As for the Romans, they sent slaves with baskets and donkeys up into the Piedmontese Alps. Not only hard work, but perilous, with the surety that much of what was amassed would melt before it reached its destination. Nevertheless, it was work that continued through different societies, sometimes in the same place. The Greeks, Romans, Arabs, and Sicilians, all in their turn, gathered Mount Etna's snow and packed it in grottoes on the slopes until it was needed.

And here's where a founding myth comes into play: the emperor Nero is credited with the invention of ice cream. Not personally, you understand, but it's supposed to have happened during his reign (54–68 AD). The claim is that Nero liked sherbet—what else but close kin to the exquisitely flavoured fruit drinks that the Arabs knew so much about. Nero's, it seems, were flavoured with honey, fruit juices, and fruit pulp, and chilled with ice. The emperor was simply following an irresistible trend. But in mythology, of course, sherbet stood in for ice cream. And it happened again.

Years ago, I came across another blended tale, part fiction, part fact. During the Third Crusade, Richard the Lion-Heart joined the siege of the city of Acre in Syria … true. Almost immediately after his arrival in June 1191, the English king fell desperately ill and was unable to leave his tent ... true. Saladin, the great Saracen leader, sent sherbet to Richard as a gesture of respect ... false. But such a civilized and civilizing gesture in the midst of a relentlessly brutal conflict, it makes you wish it happened. There is an additional fact that helps explain the genesis of the myth. According to medieval chronicles, the king's ambassadors visited Saladin in his camp on July 4, asking to buy fruit and snow. Now what do you suppose they planned to do with their purchases—make sherbet, or what Saladin would have recognized as *sharab*?

The Greek physician Galen (129–200 AD) divided illnesses into categories of hot and cold. Since fever was obviously hot, the remedy was to apply cold. Perhaps the English king's doctors were familiar with the prescription. The Arabs, whose translation of Galen was one of the routes his teachings entered Western medicine, certainly were. They used ice as a means of cooling the body, frequently advocating cold baths and chilled drinks. Saladin obliged the ambassadors by sending peaches, pears, and snow to the English king.

Richard recovered from a disease that could make hair and nails fall out, that could cause loss of sight and ultimately death—likely scurvy—and got on with the strategy and ruthlessness for which he was famous: he massacred every single one of the hostages he took when Acre fell at last into his hands on July 12. As for the sherbet, turned into a solid, it became part of ice-cream lore.

I e-mail my friend Raja Alem. She lives in Jiddah, Saudi Arabia, and is a poet, playwright, and novelist. The subject of much of her writing is the Arabia of the past. "Can you tell me anything about sherbet," I ask her, "about its connection with ice cream?"

Raja replies that her brother, Nabeel, has heard that ice cream was invented by the Syrians. Milk was left out in cold weather, and, when the milk froze, everyone thought it had gone bad. It seems they grew to like this *boza* (from the verb meaning "spoiled"). But, through a little research, I discover that *boza,* a drink made from fermented grains in Turkey, is not *buza,* Syrian ice cream. It must be a case of one word being mistaken for another, creating folklore.

As for sherbet, Raja consults her friend Suraihi, a specialist in the language. He confirms that the word *is* Arabic in origin, though it underwent Turkish modification. We're making slow but steady progress. She also consults a man she refers to simply as Professor Khazindar, who knows stories of early Mecca, the city in which she grew up. The professor doesn't find ice cream in *One Thousand and One Nights,* but he does find *sharab*—drinks of water, honey, milk, wine—there in the sensuous landscape of Scheherazade, with its genii and flying carpets, Aladdin and his lamp, Sinbad, Ali-Baba and the Forty Thieves, kings, viziers, sheiks, caliphs, slave girls, the whole gang. And this leads Raja to improvise on a theme, recalling the drink she's known all her life, one that is cold, and made with fruit and lots of sugar: *sharbat.*

The minute I see this word, I visualize the great caliphs at banquets in their palaces. Or I see the love scenes in which female slaves sip those drinks that flow in the rivers of paradise. The slave girls feed the caliphs right from their lips. In *One Thousand and One Nights,* every love scene is watered with *sharab,* and I am reminded of *sharbat* ...

Whenever I am in London, New York, or Paris, the word *sherbet* catches my eye, and a wave of homesickness washes over me. I've always wondered what this Arabic word was doing in those Western cities.

Blame it on travel, trade, and war. Putting ice in your drink as a means of beating the heat gradually spread across Europe and ultimately reached the New World too. Conversion began on the spot. Canon Pietro Casola of Milan, a pilgrim to the Holy Land, arrived in Jaffa in 1494 and was greeted by the Arabs with a sack of snow for cooling water. Fulcher of Chartres noted of the Crusaders (including himself) who settled in the territories they conquered, "We who were occidentals have now become orientals." That means they must have learned the Eastern custom of expressing the juice of fresh fruit, sweetening it to taste, passing it through a silver strainer to remove pips, pouring in water two-thirds full, and filling the container to the brim with blocks of ice or snow. Then they were ready to drink their sherbet with the best of them. That's how Englishman C. J. Wills described the elegant ceremony he witnessed in Persia in 1881. And it's pretty much the method for making a fruit drink in Raja's family today. This one is compliments of her aunt Fatma Hijji.

MULBERRY *SHARAB* OR *SHARBAT*

4 glasses of sugar
4 glasses of mulberries
Catechu water or orange flower water to taste [Catechu is astringent and derived from tropical plants.]

Put sugar in a glass pitcher.

Press mulberries and strain with a strainer.

Add juice to the sugar, stir, and leave in the refrigerator to chill. [This last the only concession to a modern world.]

To drink, pour concentrated fruit juice into a glass until one-quarter full, then add cold water and ice to the brim. Add catechu water or orange flower water to taste.

....

According to Elizabeth David, in her book *The Harvest of the Cold Months* (her title, of course, echoing the biblical reference), sherbet the drink came to Europe via Persia, Moghul India, and Turkey, in the form of "essences, pastes and powders" ready for mixing—distillations of exotic flowers and fruits, flavours of lemons, roses, violets, jasmine, redolent of the countries of their origin. (They were in no way related to the fizzy mixture of sugar, bicarbonate of soda, and cream of tartar that was introduced in England in the nineteenth century and is known today as sherbet powder.)

David points out that, in the 1570s, Francesco de' Medici, the grand duke of Tuscany, wrote to a friend asking for *ricette delle sorbette* (recipes for sherbet) in the Turkish manner. As well, she refers to the tale that icy sherbet was offered to customers in Turkish-style baths in Paris in the late sixteenth century and was available, as "made in Turkie," at a London coffee house in the seventeenth. Perhaps sherbet was also *salep,* a powder made from the root of an orchid that was mixed with orange flower water or rosewater to make a drink. In the late seventeenth century, *salep* was much enjoyed by the English, who knew it as "salop" or "saloop." In parts of the Middle East today, it's used in the making of a very chewy, elastic ice cream, which the Syrians call—you guessed it—*buza*. In Egypt, a drink from *salep* continues to be made.

Raja Alem informs me that her sister, Shadia, always associates sherbet with rosewater; every sherbet she has ever tasted was mixed with it. The sherbet was so sweet, it causes Shadia's tongue to curl even now when she thinks of it. Raja also reports that she has been looking into an Arab dictionary that contains every Arabic word along with each one's endless branching divisions and usages. Relying on the dictionary, here's how she describes the link between sherbet and the watering of a palm tree.

Al-sh-a-rabat: like a small trough, dug round the palm tree's base or trunk, to be filled with water to allow the palm tree to drink of it. The plural of the word is *sha-ra-bat*. I believe that the word *sharbat* came from those *sha-ra-bat* around the palm trees. In Egypt, *sharbat* is the drink which is distributed during weddings, when a child is born, or a student passes an examination. People mix the powder of fruits with water and distribute it in the street for every passer-by to enjoy, to pray for prosperity and for reasons to celebrate in the future.

How fascinating words are in their meandering through geography, history, and cuisine. Though Oriental sherbet didn't become solid until late in its career, it was the drink that proved a source of inspiration for European confectioners. They took it the next step: they froze it. From *sharab* and *sharbat* to *sorbetti* and *sorbets*.

However, first there was a major obstacle to overcome. Europeans had to be persuaded to let cold—freezing cold—into their bodies.

According to *The Handy Weather Answer Book*, snow that falls at a temperature near freezing is denser than snow that falls at a higher temperature, and, when it's extremely cold and the sky is clear, ice crystals may condense and fall as what is known as diamond dust. We understand snow observationally, scientifically. But our response to it is also emotional, social, subject to a wide range of influences that change over time. What appears simple turns out to be complicated.

After a winter snowfall, children throw snowballs, or they lie down on their backs and fan their arms and legs, making snow angels. And sometimes they put snow in their mouths and eat it. Winter bites back, of course. If they try to lick ice on a very cold day, their tongues can stick to the surface, frozen by their own spit. Children know this, yet someone always wants to lick.

One evening, I was watching television coverage of the winter carnival in Quebec City, and I saw visitors pouring maple syrup on clean snow, collecting the shapeless, sticky, cold mass on a popsicle stick and popping it into their mouths. The practice of pouring maple syrup on clean snow goes back to the early days of Canada, when aboriginals taught settlers to do it. And the scene caused me to remember something my brother-in-law Bill Shirley once told me. Bill grew up in Texas, and on those rare occasions when snow fell in his part of the world, his grandmother and aunts would run out and collect it "real quick, while it was still fresh, fluffy, and pure." They'd pour vanilla extract on it, and add sugar. "And we'd eat it," Bill explained.

In his charming memoir *From Stone Orchard,* writer Timothy Findley describes what he calls snow-bread, "a pioneer concoction, quintessentially Canadian," which consists of freshly fallen snow and cornmeal, baked in the oven.

....

SNOW-BREAD

Mix four or five parts of snow—depending on how fluffy it is—and one part of cornmeal. Place the mixture in greased muffin pans—we use bacon fat, for flavour—and bake for fifteen minutes at 425°F. As the melting snow provides liquid, the natural gases gathered by the falling flakes are released by heat and bubble out to provide the leavening. Serve this "snow-bread" with lots of butter and maple syrup.

....

Remarkable the ways human beings have found to make ice and snow delicious.

In another e-mail from Raja Alem, she mentions that she and her sister, Shadia, used to mix fruit with snow that they collected from outside their grandmother's door in Taif, Saudi Arabia. They'd eat it in secret because, as Raja put it, her mother would never have imagined her children devouring "the iced tears of the sky." There's the complication. The enterprise has a dark side: the taste for cold can be and has been deemed unnatural. Even dangerous by some.

The Greek physician Hippocrates (c. 460–377 BC) predicted dire consequences from giving in to it. He believed the body was a balance of humours—blood, phlegm, and black and yellow bile. The vital functions were controlled by spirits (of the heart, liver, and brain) manufactured from food. And he warned against introducing any sudden changes into this delicately balanced system. Hippocrates was convinced that his fellow citizens were throwing their bodies into perilous confusion by putting ice in their drinks. His warning cast a long shadow. Visiting Florence in 1581, Montaigne described how he put snow in his wineglass, as was the custom in the city—but only a little snow because he was feeling unwell. He was suffering from a migraine. He also had gallstones. Understandably, he was cautious about shocking his body, so he followed the golden mean.

As a scholar, Montaigne was well aware of references in classical Greek and Roman literature to the practice of icing water or wine. Montaigne knew contemporary history too. In 1568, Don Carlos, the sickly and ill-tempered, perhaps even mad, son of King Philip II of Spain, died. He'd been suffering from a high fever, during which time he poured ice water on the floor of his chamber so that he could lie naked in it. And, shortly before his death, he ate a highly spiced pastry and drank more than ten quarts of cold water. At the time, it was rumoured he'd been poisoned. But it was also suggested that he'd died from what Hippocrates had described as "suddenly throwing the body into a different state."

Seizures, blindness, paralysis, heart attack, and apoplexy were all promised repercussions from the ingestion of cold. From the sixteenth to the seventeenth century, in the midst of a medical controversy over the benefits as opposed to the disastrous, even deadly effects of consuming a frosty drink, Europeans were understandably slow to come around to the idea of taking a chance.

Not the most supportive climate, it could be argued, for the introduction of ice cream. On the other hand, maybe the debate added to ice cream's appeal, making it more attractive, titillating, exclusive—especially to those risk takers who, like children, were prepared to lick ice and get it down them too. Adventures in extreme eating are not unusual. People eat blowfish. It's just that we're not accustomed to thinking of ice cream as dangerous.

Although the French were holdouts for a long time, by the end of the sixteenth century, Henry III was cooling his wine with ice and snow. And by the end of the seventeenth, beginning of the eighteenth, Louis XIV was enjoying a form of ice cream—*Eau d'Apricots,* for example, as described in a recipe from François Massialot's *Nouvelle Instruction pour les Confitures, les Liqueurs, et les Fruits,* published in 1692. It consisted of well-ripened apricots, peeled and pitted, cut into pieces, and placed in water that had been already boiled, with a small amount of sugar. Everything sat for a while; the flavour infused. And then the mixture was beaten and poured several times from one container into another—presumably, to blend and aerate—and filtered before it was frozen. The freezing method was equally primitive. No churning, just stirring at least once to prevent the mixture from turning into a skating rink.

The result was little more than sugar, water, and a little fruit, its texture coarse, pebbly, on the whole more like faintly flavoured ice than ice cream. *Eaux glacées,* early French ices—variously made from fruit (straw-berries, raspberries, peaches); scented by flowers (violets, jasmine, jonquils)—were declared very hard indeed by later cooks and confectioners, who set out to improve them. Nevertheless, they proved popular and were served up to the king and the court in little goblets on their own special dishes—that was Massialot's suggestion, in the 1705 edition of his book, for the presentation of "a simple dessert for four people." There was even a recipe for a chocolate *eau glacée,* to be prepared in winter when fruits and flowers were nowhere to be found and His Majesty had to settle for grated chocolate infused in sugar water.

Louis was a stickler for etiquette. Sometimes he dined in public, when all who were properly dressed could file past his table, and sometimes in private, when courtiers and servants were allowed to stand and watch. Only his brother, who was known as Monsieur, sat down to join him. Oh, to have been one of the watchers the moment Louis XIV—whom Saint-Simon, in his memoirs, described as a figure of great dignity—sampled his first ice. Maybe the king licked it at the outset. But there must have been a crackle and squeal when his teeth pierced an ice crystal or two. Clearly he enjoyed the confection: he had a pair of ice houses built at Versailles to supply his needs. But ice cream fit for a king had a long way to go.

Old recipes are like footprints in the snow: they indicate many paths taken and sometimes rejected. Recipes are translated and adapted. The writers of them travel too, learning techniques in other countries that they take home and domesticate or, settling abroad, put into action in their new home. It was long thought that Catherine de' Medici—who, in 1533, married the duke d'Orléans, the future Henry II of France—took recipes for ices and a retinue of Italian confectioners along with her. But the first recipe in French doesn't appear until 1674, in Nicholas Lemery's *Recueil de curiositéz rares et nouvelles de plus admirables effets de la nature,* published in English, in 1694, as *Modern Curiosities of Art and Nature.*

As for the Italian connection, not until the same year, 1694, were recipes for *sorbetti* published, in Antonio Latini's second edition of *Lo Scalco alla Moderna* (The Modern Steward). The *sorbetti,* claimed Latini, were the marvellous consistency of sugar and snow. At least one French confectioner, L. Audiger, announced in his steward's handbook, *La Maison Réglée* (1692), that he'd been to Italy to study how to make them. Surprising, then, that the kind prepared for Louis XIV were reputed to have been so hard and inferior. It had to have been the novelty that delighted the king. At Marly, the king's favourite summer retreat, at the end of a grand fête celebrating the birth of his great-grandson, pale pink, green, yellow, and ·

white ices were served. On that day, August 14, 1704, the fortunes of ice cream were surely rising.

Cinnamon, orange blossoms, coffee, muscat grapes, pistachios, pineapples, almonds, vanilla, cloves, and other waters distilled from seeds (fennel, for example) supplied the flavouring. Cream, milk, and egg yolks entered the mix.

The vocabulary for ingredients and measurements reveal different imaginations at work in different countries— and sometimes on the same recipe because, bluntly put, sometimes it was filched. Convention in the past was banditry; attribution was cavalier. The mighty Handel was accused by his contemporaries of stealing from other composers, prompting a certain John Potter to observe, in 1762, that a composer, like "the curious bee, sucks sweets from every flower." What an apt gustatory metaphor. Merely substitute *cook* for *composer* and you have in your sights Vincente La Chapelle, chief cook to the duke of Chesterfield. He lifted major portions of his 1733 book, *The Modern Cook,* from *Massialot's Le Cuisinier Royal et Bourgeois* (1691). As for the exceptionally popular Mrs. Hannah Glasse, she could plagiarize with the best of them. It's been suggested that, in her second edition of *The Art of Cookery, Made Plain and Easy* (1751), she was merely reporting what she'd been told or read about how to make her famous raspberry cream ice; the recipe is so sketchy. It seems Mrs. Glasse was determined to get into the game one way or another.

History has a messy and tangled underbrush, where competition is fierce and ambitions are at stake. But if the question of authorship is put aside, and if you judge by the number of recipes in cookbooks that came out in Europe during one small window of time—fifty years or so, from the end of the seventeenth to the middle of the eighteenth century—it's remarkable how quickly the appetite for the new treat was whetted and fulfilled.

The age of ice cream was well and truly under way, best illustrated by a 1768 cookbook entirely devoted to it, *L'Art de Bien Faire les Glaces d'Office,* by M. Emy— 240 pages brimming with recipes for apricot, violet, rose, chocolate, and caramel (among others) ices as well as ice cream. "Food fit for the gods," the reader was told. Emy included theological and philosophical explanations on various aspects of the process, including the freezing of water. But a most charming expression of the sublimity of ice cream lies at the very beginning of the book. The engraving on the frontispiece shows a pastoral scene so beloved of the time, in which angels—putti, actually,

LITTLE ANGELS MAKING ICE CREAM

little cupid caterers—freeze and dole out portions into individual goblets, while one of their company flies heavenward, carrying a platter to the deities, two of whom recline on a cloud, awaiting their pleasure.

So there isn't a single inventor, Ur-chef, Ur-cook, Ur-confectioner of ice cream. At least not in Europe. At least not on historical record. Instead, a bevy of individuals are associated with it, and their names have been largely forgotten, except by food historians. Still, Yeats talks about the "rage for order." And since there's something in us that yearns for a story with a beginning as well as a middle, I've saved the most persistent myth about ice cream for the end. It purports to deal with origins. Then again, maybe it isn't entirely a myth. I'm going to hedge my bets.

"In Xanadu did Kubla Khan/ A stately pleasure-dome decree ..." The famous opening lines of Samuel Taylor Coleridge's poem "Kubla Khan." It's the very same pleasure-dome described by the thirteenth-century merchant and traveller Marco Polo, who claimed he'd actually seen it, been in it, marvelled at it. As the Venetian writes, the pleasure-dome was a magnificent reed palace set within an enclosed garden. The reed columns were topped by gilt dragons, whose tails wrapped around the columns and whose heads and massive paws supported the roof. The columns were fastened together by nails and silk cords, so that the great khan could erect and strike his summer palace at will. So much wondrous detail is provided in *The Travels of Marco Polo,* you'd think he would have reported if he'd seen anything as remarkable as ice cream being made in China. And yet, according to the myth, he's supposed to have witnessed exactly that, seen it sold on the streets there, furthermore, and carried the recipe back with him to Italy. The myth is specific in some tellings. It was a frozen-milk dessert, resembling modern sherbet, that he found. But no mention of such a treat exists in his *Travels.*

Marco Polo does testify to the drinking of *kumiss,* fermented milk that was part of the Mongol diet. And he explains that Kublai Khan bred a large number of snow-white horses, and that milk from the mares could be drunk only by people related to the khan or by warriors who won a victory for him. This custom of drinking mare's milk relates perhaps to a recipe dating back much earlier. The T'ang rulers in China (618–907 AD) took pleasure in a mysterious dish that was made from *kumiss* (from the milk of mares or, alternatively, cows, goats, or water buffalo) mixed with rice, camphor, dragon brain fragments, and dragon eyeball powder (whatever these last two ingredients may be). The mixture was placed in a metal container and submerged in an ice pool. But was this "clear wind rice," as it's been called, frozen or merely thoroughly chilled? Then there are the lines from the Sung dynasty poet Yang Wanli (1127–1206 AD):

It looks so greasy but still has a crisp texture,
It appears congealed and yet it seems to float,
Like jade, it breaks at the bottom of the dish;
As with snow, it melts in the light of the sun.

You'll find this poem in *Frozen Desserts* by Caroline Liddell and Robin Weir, who explain that it is a description of frozen milk. A description involving similes, I note, not steps in a recipe. Was this an early form of ice cream? Did ice cream in fact originate in China? Possibly … perhaps … probably.

The real question is, Whom does this founding myth serve? With regard to Marco Polo and his association with ice cream, I'd say the Italians stand to benefit. The myth has circulated in the West, not in China. I think it's a kind of ancestor story for Italians, who have been and still are makers of superlative ice cream. Antiquity provides them with a certain cachet; it's a tried-and-true formula. For example, Europeans desperately wanted to believe they were descended from Aeneas, who was supposed to have escaped the burning city of Troy when it fell to the Greeks. In his epic *The Aeneid,* Virgil made the case for the Romans and, therefore, for the Italians. France and England had their own versions, just so everybody could boast of a glamorous and heroic past. It was called "the matter of Troy." So I'm considering the myth of Marco Polo and ice cream as "the matter of China."

In a way, his travel narrative qualifies as myth. It was considered a fabrication in his own time and was nicknamed *Il Milione* (The Million Lies). And it's given modern Sinologists pause. Tea drinking and foot binding— crucial aspects of Chinese culture Marco Polo could be expected to have observed—are not given even a passing glance. He makes no reference to the Great Wall either. Marco Polo's name does not appear in the contemporary "Annals of the Empire" *(Yuan Shih),* in which the names of foreign visitors were recorded. These omissions have raised doubts whether he ever reached China at all, instead relying on others' accounts of it, simply appropriating or inventing whatever he chose.

But let's give Marco Polo a break. Medieval travel accounts were carryalls, accommodating as much fiction as fact, and anything that was included in them could easily have been plagiarized. The following description stayed with me from the moment I read it in the enormously popular fourteenth-century *Mandeville's Travels*. In Ethiopia, says the fictional John Mandeville, "there be folk that have but one foot … that foot is so large that it shades all the body against the sun, when they want to lie down and rest." By comparison, Marco Polo's account of what he saw and experienced in the world beyond Europe is remarkably restrained.

He did have wiggle room, however, and he used it. Claiming to have arrived at Kublai Khan's summer palace, Xanadu *(Shang-du)*, in 1275, he presents this scene of feasting there. The great khan's table is raised above floor level, and on the floor are "cups filled with milk"—*kumiss*, likely—"wine, and other delicious drinks." Magicians make the cups rise up and fly to the khan and, when he has drunk from them, return dutifully to their place on the floor—as witnessed by ten thousand people, Marco Polo insists, and, therefore, "absolutely true."

Now, any man who fashioned the above scene could have easily invented one involving the eating of ice cream.

It would have been an astonishing revelation to his countrymen, especially when he told them that, in Kublai Khan's palace, ice cream flew through the air with the drinks. Merely that it was frozen through and through would have been enough to confound them. In addition, if he had the recipe in his pocket, he surely would have been their benefactor. But he did not and he was not. And, since he had no acquaintance with ice cream after all, later generations simply made it up. It's reasonable to assume that an anonymous Italian, with a lot to gain, invented the myth at a date unknown. And so the myth persists that Marco Polo delivered ice cream from the exotic East to the grateful West.

To get a Chinese perspective, I ask my acupuncturist, Yuhua Wang, "Do you eat ice cream in your country?"

"Ice cream's only for children," she says.

There are few commercial freezers in China, and very few Chinese have home freezers. Even though they can buy ice cream, including Western brands, primarily in big cities like Beijing and Shanghai, by and large they have a very different and more restricted experience of it.

"It's not like in the West. We give milk only to children," she says. I can almost hear her wrinkle her nose. Unlike the Mongols, a high percentage of Chinese today are lactose intolerant.

I'm lying on my back with needles between my toes, in my ankles, knees, arms, neck, temples, beside my nostrils, and across the crown of my head. Yuhua trained in Beijing (Kublai Khan's capital too, bearing the name of Cambalac, according to Marco Polo), and she can provide traditional, ancient terms for the healing work she does with needles, sometimes pressing them up and down, moving them back and forth, or twisting them. Needles are tigers. The energy is a fish taking the hook. She speaks in images as old as acupuncture, whose beginning is buried in legend. But she's silent when I ask her if she's ever heard the story that ice cream originated in the China of Kublai Khan. Eventually, trying to be helpful, she volunteers that she remembers many time-honoured folk tales about rice, not about ice cream.

In the realm of history, not myth, the fact is, Western ice cream was introduced into China in the twentieth century. In 1909, according to *Ice and Refrigeration,* an American trade journal, crowds in Canton gathered around a street vendor with a freezer. For a culture accustomed to iced rather than icy foods, American-style ice cream was a phenomenon.

Just imagine this scene taking place in Kublai Khan's summer pleasure-dome. You know enough now to separate truth from fable. The royal acupuncturist has worked on an injury the emperor sustained in falling from one of his snow-white mares. Rejoicing that he's not badly hurt, the court has assembled. The cups have flown, been emptied, and returned to their place on the floor. But the khan is feeling the heat—it's a sultry day; the *kumiss* has gone to his head. He strokes his sculpted, bifurcated beard and ponders.

Then he gives orders to his royal chef to bring in a batch of that … that T'ang delicacy … what's it called? … Oh yes, "clear wind rice," the milk dessert that floats like jade and melts in the sun. The great khan is feeling generous. He commands that enough be provided for his warriors, including the Venetian who's recently entered his service.

As for Marco Polo, he seems far more preoccupied with the paper money that's been instituted throughout the empire than he is with its frozen delicacy. But a merchant would be thus preoccupied. In fact, Marco Polo is astonished. He's never seen paper money before, and he tells himself to remember the look and feel of it, how light it is to carry. He completely ignores the importance of the imperial ice stores, from which ice is brought to chill the food and drinks he's been enjoying, unaware that ice has been used to cool houses of the court as long ago as the T'ang dynasty and probably longer. He is oblivious to the fact that the Chinese have been collecting and storing ice for thousands of years. It's recorded in a poem from around 1100 BC in the collection of food canons *(Shih Ching),* and it's another of the notable omissions in *The Travels of Marco Polo.*

THE HARVESTING OF ICE

As Thoreau observed, ice is "a fit subject for contemplation." He was intrigued enough to wonder why a bucket of water could turn rancid but, frozen, "remains sweet forever," as he watched men come to Walden Pond in successive Januarys, 1846 and 1847, bringing farm tools to harvest ice that looked to him like "solidified azure." They marked and carved it, divided it into cakes, ten thousand tons' worth. They stacked and covered it with hay and boards to keep the air out.

"At first," he wrote in *Walden,* "it looked like a vast blue fort or Valhalla; but when they began to tuck the coarse meadow hay in the crevices, and this became covered with rime and icicles, it looked like a venerable moss-grown and hoary ruin, built of azure-tinted marble, the abode of Winter, that old man we see in the almanac."

A remarkable ice house, according to Thoreau, that, even though it had no roof and was exposed to the sun, didn't thaw completely until September 1848. The icemen took what they wanted and shipped it off, abandoning the rest for nature to deal with in its own inimitable way. Slowly, the "vast blue fort" would melt down to its foundations, hay and boards left behind to rot. When Thoreau looked out from the cabin he built on Walden Pond, the harvesting of ice and snow was at its peak commercially, but it was also coming to an end. A little more than fifty years later, in 1917, the first electric refrigerators were being manufactured in France and the United States. Nature was bypassed. That scene on Walden Pond would not happen again.

Some things pass, and others remain the same. I heard once that one-third of the earth's surface is covered with ice. Throughout history and some of prehistory, human beings have harvested it from mountains, lakes, rivers, and ponds, hauled and stored and used it to refresh, cool, even medicate themselves. And they've told tales about it. You could argue that ice cream was just a by-product of more serious "contemplation," the *study* of cold, the science of freezing.

But science can't do justice to the *taste* for cold, the appeal of ice cream that does not pass, the sybaritic moment of consumption when cold turns to sweetness and, warmed by the body, slides down the throat, to the most cordial of receptions. The cycle of the seasons turns from winter to summer with every bite, over and over again. Ice cream is the release of flavour captured ingeniously, vivaciously, in ice. That's what the taste for cold is all about.

2

MILK FROM WHICH ALL BLESSINGS FLOW

Contemplate the cow for a moment. The Holstein cow specifically—you know, the black and white one. The Holstein supplies most of the milk that's used for making ice cream in the United States, the country that manufactures most of the ice cream in the world. In fact, it's a huge industry there: about 9 percent of American milk production is dedicated to it. And consider the name "ice cream." Milk (with its cream content) is the defining ingredient. For many people on the globe, ice cream isn't ice cream without it. Just ask its most numerous and enthusiastic consumers: New Zealanders first, followed by Americans, Australians, and Canadians.

Yet, in 1961, American Reuben Mattus wanted his customers to think of *Denmark* when he launched his ice cream under the bizarre brand name of Häagen-Dazs. Invented by his wife, Rose, the name was bogus, especially the umlaut, which doesn't exist in the Danish language. The label's claim of a high percentage of butterfat, on the other hand, was true. That's what "superpremium" signifies, and Häagen-Dazs was the first superpremium company on the map. In contrast to other commercial varieties that had little milk and less cream, and were packaged in bulky economy-size cartons, Häagen-Dazs made its debut in pint-sized containers and sold initially in small stores in Manhattan.

So what's in a name? Mattus was banking on the Danish reputation for quality. His ice cream cost twice as much and was worth every penny. In the 1960s, '70s, and '80s, Häagen-Dazs proved to be the fastest-growing ice-cream company of them all. Now in twenty-eight countries, it's owned by the giant corporation Pillsbury. The odd and improvised name has stuck, and the butter-fat content remains high.

However, if you think Mattus was the first to connect ice cream with a country as a selling point, think again. In 1691, the Frenchman François Massialot (whom you met in chapter 1) created a recipe using cream and milk, sugar, and egg yolks that he blended together. Then he froze the mixture in a cheese-shaped mould and called it *fromage à l'Angloise.*

The adjective *Angloise,* which is surely an older form of *anglaise,* acknowledges a fact of history that was also a matter of taste. While the French and Italians of the time tended to prefer water ices, "iced cream" was more popular with the English. Of course, the French and Italians gradually changed their allegiance. At least, they became experts at making ice cream that exploited the qualities of milk. After all, it leads to a lush, richer ice cream—you can tell which side I'm on.

But centuries before Europeans were even considering which side *they* were on, South Asians had already decided in favour of milk.

The next time you're looking at a picture of—or are lucky enough to visit—the Taj Mahal, you might keep in mind that Shah Jahan, who had this extraordinarily beautiful tomb built in the seventeenth century to honour his dead wife, might have known something about ice cream as well. Legend has it that the Moghuls introduced ice cream into

India. They were the descendants of Genghis Khan and Timur Lane (Timberlaine); their name comes from the Persian for "Mongol," and a vast part of their territory included much of Persia, Afghanistan, and the north of India. Perhaps they brought the recipe with them when they invaded India in 1526, by way of Afghanistan. Perhaps they discovered it when they settled there. All this is supposition, coloured even more brightly by the following tall tale.

In the far distant past, a Mongol was riding his horse in the Himalayas, carrying a sack made from the intestines of a goat and filled with yak's milk. The temperature dropped below freezing in the mountains, and, as the horse galloped, the yak's milk was churned by the vibration. The result was the world's first ice cream. This is an Eastern founding tale. But, during their three hundred years of rule in India, the Moghuls were nomadic horsemen no longer. They travelled on the backs of elephants, wore silks and brocades, sat on the Peacock Throne, established an empire and a dynasty. Shah Jahan's illustrious predecessor, the emperor Akbar—whose name means "Greatest"—ruled from 1556 until 1605.

It was Akbar who commanded Abul Fazl Allami to write the *Ain-i-Akbari*, or *The Institutions of Akbar*, in which it appears there's evidence of ice cream—*kulfi*, that is, prepared in the royal kitchens, using *khoya,* milk that is boiled slowly over a fire until it is greatly reduced and becomes the essence of itself. Although it's impossible to know precisely when the recipe was invented, it is considered, as with so many dishes the Moghuls ushered into Indian cooking, to be of Persian origin. The presence of almonds and pistachios in the mix, even rosewater, and the use of gold and silver leaf as decoration reveal the Moghul touch. *Kulfi* dates back at least to the Moghul emperors, who had hundreds of cooks to do their bidding, and that included the making of ice cream.

Traditionally, *kulfi* was frozen in little conical moulds sealed with dough—it still is, for that matter, if the maker is being traditional. The moulds are put into earthenware pots surrounded by ice and salt and are pretty much left to their own devices. In her *Illustrated Indian Cookery,* Madhur Jaffrey explains that, when she was growing up, *kulfi* was never made at home. Small wonder; the process is inordinately time consuming. Jaffrey recalls that people would hire the local *kulfi-wallah,* or "ice-cream man," to produce for the many guests at a wedding banquet, for example. Every now and then, the *kulfi-wallah* would stir the hundreds of moulds in the hundreds of pots he had brought with him, a kind of minimal churning for a massive undertaking. But the result is worth it. In their book *Frozen Desserts,* Caroline Liddell and Robin Weir describe the splendour of a formal presentation. The *kulfi* is set on its base on the plate, sliced in half across the top, then in half again, so that it splays out like a four-pointed flower or star, the tips shining from the gold or silver leaf that crowns them.

But there are more casual ways to enjoy it. I head off to a restaurant in the city where I live to encounter everyday *kulfi.* The restaurant is in a neighbourhood known as Little India, several city blocks that, on a warm summer evening, release fragrant smells of coriander, ginger, curry. Grocery stores sell ghee and ripe mangoes. Women wear saris or the ballooning trousers and blouse of Pakistan. The specialty of the Lahore Tikka House is, obviously, *tikka,* meat deliciously seasoned and cooked on skewers. But it also has what I'm seeking. When I arrive, the Pakistani restaurant is crowded with families enjoying lunch.

"Hello, my name is Alnoor Sayani," the manager says when he joins me at the table. I've asked to speak with him. I want to know whether ice cream is made on the premises. "Yes," he says, "and you have to have strong arms to do this job. *Kulfi* takes almost a whole day to make because you have to keep on stirring and stirring."

"You don't use an electric ice-cream maker?"

"Absolutely not." He's emphatic. "It's done the old-fashioned way, and it's been going on for thousands of years, from generation to generation. One of my uncles gave us the traditional recipe. You keep on boiling the milk, boiling the milk, until it becomes the texture of thick porridge, what we call *khoya*." He confirms that *kulfi* is frequently served at weddings. "But if you go to Lahore, in Pakistan, you'll find a whole street of stores and vendors of ice cream—that's all you'll get on that street," he says. "The idea is to walk and have a *kulfi* on a stick at the same time."

Sounds familiar. In Italy, in the early evening, people stroll and eat a cone of *gelato;* the walkabout is called the *passeggiata*. In Spain too—kids and adults out for a *paseo*. Lots of people enjoying ice cream. Common ground.

"Here, try this!" Mr. Sayani hands me a *kulfi* on a stick. It's wide at the base, rising to a narrow tip—the shape of its conical mould. He explains that flavours can be added—pistachio, mango, passion fruit—but the plain original is the best. "This is the *khoya kulfi,* the real McCoy," he tells me. Cream-coloured because the milk has been reduced, it's also very dense, very heavy. So it's supported by what looks like a chopstick. Turns out that's exactly what it is. Mr. Sayani has improvised from another culture.

Then I have my first lick, and it takes me by surprise. The ice cream is thick and especially cold on the tongue. It also tastes and smells intensely of milk. Maybe too much of milk. I'm not accustomed to such concentration. It's unlike any ice cream that I've experienced.

Kulfi doesn't seem to have made concessions to the West, the way sherbet has done, allowing itself to be frozen and reconceptualized. I remember seeing a 1920s menu from one of the British officers' clubs in India under the Raj. Stressing its culinary chic, the entire menu was in French. The dessert, therefore, was listed as *"parfait praline."* What do you suppose? Was *kulfi* considered too native when the British moved in and deposed the last Moghul emperor in 1858? Or when Queen Victoria was proclaimed empress of India in 1876? Was it simply that the milky taste was alien to English middle-class memsahibs who joined their husbands and set up households all over the country in a fiercely chauvinist way? Perhaps it just comes down to the fact that ice cream was no longer a novelty by the time the British ruled India. And the Indian method of making *kulfi* was so labour intensive.

There is, however, an extremely interesting aspect to the myth of the Mongol warrior and his horse. In Marco Polo's account of his travels, he described seeing armies of nomads milking their mares. He called them Tartars, meaning "Mongolians" or "Turks." They boiled the mare's milk, skimmed off the cream that rose to the top, dried the cream in the sun, and then, with a specified amount of water, put it into a "bottle." When they were ready to use it, they rode with the bottle on horseback, allowing the contents to be "violently shaken" (Polo's words), from which a thin porridge resulted, and they had it for dinner. A practical matter, nothing more. But mythologizing turned the porridge into ice cream—just as a variant of the same myth placed ice cream at the court of the Mongolian Kublai Khan. It's part and parcel of the impulse to romanticize the dessert, which emerges, like the drawing of an elephant in a medieval bestiary, as a pastiche, not a fact.

Just when I think I've learned as much as I can about the fortunes of *kulfi* in the West, a friend arrives at my door with a plastic container he's bought locally. "Pistachio *kulfi*—for your research," he volunteers. The blurb on the side of the container advertises the pistachio *kulfi* as "truly exotic … made in the traditional style with

wholesome cream … strands of saffron and cardamom"
mixed in with the nuts. This *kulfi* is not as dense as the
kind I had in the restaurant. The company also promotes
other flavours and styles from the East: saffron, mango,
coconut, lychee, soursop, green tea, date, fig.

But for the purist, there's something that can be
ordered from the Net. It is akin to the Mongol warrior's ice
cream in a bottle—except it's ice cream in a gym bag. All
the ingredients necessary arrive in the bag. It just has to be
attached to a horse, a boat, possibly jet skis. Vibration does
the rest in forty minutes. The Westernizing has begun, I
guess, as a more recent recipe, with its shortcuts, reveals.
Here it is, as submitted by Simmi Gupta to allrecipes.com.

....

KULFI

1 1/4 cups evaporated milk

1 1/4 cups sweetened condensed milk

1 (16 oz.) container frozen whipped topping, thawed

4 slices white bread, torn into pieces

1/2 teaspoon ground cardamom

Combine evaporated milk, condensed milk and
whipped topping in a blender and blend in pieces of
bread until smooth.

Pour mixture into a 13- × 9-inch baking dish or two plastic ice cube trays, sprinkle with cardamom and freeze for 8 hours or overnight.

For extra flavour, add a few drops of rosewater or ground pistachios.

....

It would be impossible to know for sure who was first among Europeans to add milk to ice cream. Probably the Italians. In cultures where milk was already an important part of the cuisine, its inclusion in ice cream was inevitable. Among the earliest evidence is an anonymous book—Neapolitan, probably seventeenth century—called *Brieve e Nuovo Modo da farsi ogni sorte di Sorbette con facilità* (A Brief and New Way to Make Easily All Kinds of Sorbets). It contains spectacular recipes. One calls for reduced milk (interestingly, as in *kulfi*), scented with orange flower water and cream of cinnamon, thickened with butter and cream, to which is added a minced candied-pumpkin sweetmeat. Another calls for milk flavoured with pounded cinnamon bark and cream of cinnamon, and is thickened again with the same candied-pumpkin sweetmeat—obviously a Neapolitan favourite. This recipe is given the poetic name *sorbetta d'Aurora* (sunrise sorbet), which must refer to the streaks of orange through it, as delicate as the morning sky.

What's so striking about such recipes is how they luxuriate in the presence of milk, coupling it with ingredients that would make the cooking and freezing an ambitious adventure and the eating a gourmet delight. Even reading the recipes is delectable. But there was a medical case to be made too.

In 1775, Dr. Filippo Baldini, a Neapolitan physician, devoted a portion of his treatise on the uses of ice and snow to *sorbetti,* in which he delineated the virtues of milk from various animals. Ices made with ass's milk were judged to be useful as blood purifiers. Those made from goat's milk were important in the treatment of diarrhea and hemorrhages. Sheep's milk ices were advised for diarrhea, dysentery, and hemorrhage, as well as for emaciation. Sorbets made with cow's milk were said to be helpful for those with paralysis and scurvy. And there were many more ailments for which ice cream could be prescribed. If nothing else, it brought comfort to the patients by caressing their palate and bucking their spirit.

But it's obvious that theory could elevate the status of a luxury food to one with more serious pretensions, all because of the presence of milk, which lent to ice cream its own panoply of meaning—health, nourishment, and more, as the following tale illustrates.

This is a milkmaid's tale. In 1782, on the grounds of Versailles, near the Petit Trianon chateau, a farmhouse was built for Queen Marie Antoinette. As the design expanded to include thatched cottages, a pigeon house, and a dairy too, it evolved into a toy hamlet at the edge of a pond. A dozen buildings in all; some ten of them survive today. This was *"le hameau de la Reine,"* the village where Marie Antoinette liked to play milkmaid in a rustic scene she commissioned and created.

Everything was *à la mode,* of course, which meant a studied simplicity for the queen. She had a point to make. Accompanied by her small entourage, she was withdrawing from the ceremonial stuffiness of the palace, retreating more and more to the Petit Trianon and her village. There, she and her friends could engage in a masquerade, pretend to be common folk—millers, pigeon keepers, fishermen, farmers, and, last but not least, royal milkmaid. Dressing up or, more accurately, dressing down. In 1783, Marie Antoinette was painted wearing a muslin blouse, without a wig, and with her hair unpowdered. The point was made.

Given what happened to her, it's ironic that the queen of France was an advocate of the simple life. But she was not alone. In an age of pre-Romantic sentimentality, humble virtues were praised by both writers and artists in France. Chardin was painting scenes of quiet domesticity. Rousseau's influence was growing. In his novel *Emile,* published in 1762, Rousseau praised nature as the source of all that was good and healthy, even advocating a plain, wholesome diet in which milk figured prominently. He provided a model. It wasn't so much that the queen and her courtiers imagined they were being virtuous when they sipped cups of milk in her dairy. Without a pinch of conscience, they'd as easily polish off *glaces à la crème* or *glaces en beurre* (made with up to twenty egg yolks to a pint of cream and half a pound of sugar). They were pretend villagers, after all. However, their highly stylized, indeed artificial, pastoralism *did* envelop milk in its embrace.

Pastoralism wasn't new. Shepherds and shepherdesses had been gambolling through lines of English poetry, for example, since the Renaissance. "Come live with me and be my love," as Marlowe's "passionate shepherd" sings— preferably in Arcadia, that remote and mountainous region in ancient Greece, that legendary never-never land of the bucolic. Yet at Versailles, pastoralism was given a local setting. And Marie Antoinette was on to something when she cast herself in the role of the milkmaid.

All you have to do is look at the continuous tradition in paintings to realize that it's a domestic world, a female world, a natural world that is being expressed, from Jan Vermeer's milkmaid in the seventeenth century (who stands pouring a thin stream from a pitcher, bathed in the light of an open window) to Winslow Homer's nineteenth-century version (with flowers at her feet, carrying her bucket and three-legged stool, as she gazes contemplatively into the distance). Goya painted the milkmaid, Gainsborough too. The figure had appeal far beyond the doomed society of the French court.

And, by extension, ice cream shared in the mythology surrounding the milkmaid: innocence, purity, above all, pastoralism—even when it was tested by contaminated milk carried in open pails through city streets (Tobias Smollett used this detail in his novel *The Expedition of Humphry Clinker*) or by ice cream made in the most unsanitary of conditions (Mrs. A. B. Marshall denounced this practice). Both examples occurred in London almost a century apart. Obviously, reality had to catch up with the mythology.

OLD-FASHIONED ICE-CREAM MAKER

My sister has sent me a photograph of an oil painting she did for a member of her husband's family. On an old wooden farmhouse table sits an oaken bucket, the same kind of bucket in which the milkmaid traditionally collected milk and churned butter. Just visible over the top is part of the metal canister inside the bucket. The crank is still inserted through the canister, though the dasher has been removed. It leans against the bucket. On one side is a jar of strawberry preserves, with the lid removed and a spoon resting on it; on the other are an ice pick and a few fresh strawberries. Homemade, hand-cranked ice cream has just been made. Some of it slathers down the dasher onto a plate, the first and most delicious sampling to taste. Behind the table and the bucket is a bright blue sky.

To my knowledge, my sister has never hand-cranked homemade ice cream, and yet, as an artist, she's participating in the romance of it. I telephone her in Texas and ask: "Gwyn, what do you associate with home-cranked ice cream?"

"When I did the painting, it was June, and it was hot. And I thought, Why don't I forget this picture and just go out and buy some ice cream?" She laughs. "We made it once or twice here on the patio, and I had a go at it." So I'm wrong. My sister *has* been initiated into hand-cranking.

"Tell me more about the blue-sky background," I say.

"Well, since making ice cream is an old-fashioned thing to do, I guess it symbolizes the simpler life." My sister pauses. "I don't remember anybody making ice cream when we were growing up."

"Maybe that's because we lived in a city and not on a farm." I mention to her that the ice-cream maker she painted was invented by a woman.

"Really, that's interesting," she says. "How many women do you know in history who are credited as inventors?" Which opens a new scenario, in which the milkmaid has to fight for her rights.

On September 9, 1843, Nancy M. Johnson received a U.S. patent for what she called her artificial freezer. Of course the Patent Office assumed the inventor was a man and addressed her mail accordingly. So Nancy M. Johnson wrote back, complaining that she'd had difficulty getting her letter of acknowledgment from the post office; it had been directed to a Mr. N. M. Johnson.

Actually, a man *did* beat her to the punch, but not in her own country. The first British patent for an ice-cream maker had been issued just a few months before her patent was approved, to Thomas Masters, confectioner to the Royal Zoological Gardens and the Royal Polytechnic Institution. The French had patented models as early as 1829. At any rate, it seems fitting that a woman invented a machine that basically derived from a bucket down on the farm. Johnson's ice-cream maker was more efficient than the old "pot-freezer," which was a start-and-stop operation, unless you could stir the mix at the same time as you turned or shook the pot up and down in a container of salt and ice. On Johnson's machine, the crank turned the dasher continuously; the dasher stirred the mixture non-stop, moving ice particles that formed on the wall of the canister in towards the centre, resulting in a smoother, lighter, creamier ice cream.

Johnson's patent listed a Philadelphia address, as Anne Cooper Funderburg points out in her book *Chocolate, Strawberry, and Vanilla*. But it may be inevitable that, given nineteenth-century gender politics, nobody cared to preserve much of her biography or even to corroborate certain basic facts. She's been described as the wife of a naval officer, someone who lived in Washington, D.C.— or was it New Jersey? Some accounts give the date of her patent as 1846, though the month, day, and year— September 9, 1843—are clearly legible on the patent. For some reason, Nancy M. and her husband (there *was* a Mr. Johnson) signed over rights to Williams and Co. for a mere $1,500—or was it $200? And there the trail ends. Except that, on May 30, 1848, William G. Young of Baltimore received his own patent for an ice-cream machine that was basically Johnson's design—new and improved, he claimed, because the canister as well as the dasher turned, providing more aeration. Young presented his machine to the U.S. Patent Office as the Johnson Patent Ice-Cream Freezer and advertised it as such.

It's clear that Mrs. Nancy M. Johnson herself never craved public recognition. Nor was she concerned with earning much money from her invention. We may assume that she retreated gracefully into Victorian domesticity,

Jacob Fussell was a Quaker, an abolitionist, a friend of Abraham Lincoln, a philanthropist, and a fiercely determined capitalist. He had no doubts: commercial and wholesale was the way of the future. One hundred years after he went into ice-cream wholesaling, the trade was profitable nationwide and celebrating a high point. In Baltimore, in June 1951, Fussell's daughter (then eighty-four) unveiled a plaque at the Exeter Street premises where it all began. Free ice cream was supplied to the city's children. Actors Piper Laurie and Tony Curtis were crowned "Sweethearts of the Ice Cream Industry." And Senator Herbert R. O'Connor praised the industry as a uniquely American achievement, the happy result of individual initiative and private enterprise. I suppose you could argue this is a male model of success as opposed to a female one—up from the dairy into big business.

"The trouble is," my sister says, "now we're afraid of a lot of commercial ice cream and the stuff they're putting into it."

"That's where Nancy M. Johnson and her ice-cream machine comes in," I tell her. "Rather than buying it, people have gone back to making it, so they have control over the ingredients and the process."

"Except they're not cranking a handle on a canister in a bucket. They're using an electric ice-cream maker."

"Sure," I say, "but I'm talking about the spirit in the machine, the same spirit that made you want to paint it."

When I hang up the telephone, I still have the photograph of my sister's painting sitting in front of me. Ice cream as still life. And, staring at it, I realize that some people, these days, *are* using the bucket-and-crank method, resorting to old-fashioned technology precisely because it *is* old fashioned. And if they don't make the ice cream themselves, they look to someone who'll do it in a manner they can trust. That's what Ben Cohen and Jerry Greenfield were banking on when they opened their first ice-cream parlour, in Burlington, Vermont, in 1978.

It was called Ben and Jerry's Homemade and was heavy on "particulates," chunky candy bits in the ice cream, a relatively new idea at the time. (The repertoire soon expanded to include other "add-ins"—nuts, cookie bits, fudge, marshmallows, toffee, fruit, pretzels, you name it.) But equally important was the image the owners fashioned for their parlour. It was consciously old fashioned. At the opening, while a honky-tonk piano tinkled out familiar tunes in the background, a whole lot of churning was going on at an antique ice-cream maker.

Customers lined up, waiting expectantly for fresh ice cream, and they even got to lick the dasher.

Finding a niche and filling a need was a well thought out market strategy. As entrepreneurs, Ben and Jerry knew how to exploit the "back to nature" movement. Soon they were selling wholesale to local markets and franchising scoop shops. In 1985, they set out across the United States in a vehicle known as the Cowmobile, offering free samples of their ice cream wherever they went. When the Cowmobile caught fire and burned outside Cleveland, Ohio, Ben (who was responsible for promotions) cleverly remarked that it "looked like a giant Baked Alaska."

The two friends' ice-cream business was enormously successful. And since distribution was the name of the game, in August 2000, Ben and Jerry's Homemade, Inc., joined forces with the multinational Unilever. But the original little company that could assured everyone that the founders' spirit and "mission" would prevail. It would still keep real cows, grazing out front of the ice-cream parlour in Burlington, Vermont. Ben and Jerry's pictures would still be found on ecologically sensitive unbleached paper containers, which would still bear witty, hand-cranked names on them—Jerry's Jubilee, Blondies Are a

Swirl's Best Friend, Cherry Garcia, Kaberry Kaboom. Under the banner "International," the rhetoric on the website today remains enthusiastic about bringing "euphoric" ice cream to "folks around the world," from Israel to Europe to all of North America.

A commercial ice-cream company that keeps the idealism of its product alive, the association with pastoralism intact, is rare. Old Macdonald couldn't be more grateful. So often exploitation is involved in the conduct of big business, as Jacob Fussell could attest. Back in the nineteenth century, when Fussell was dealing in milk, "swill dairies" were common—cows were kept in stables, never got out to feed on grass, and were given "swill" instead, usually waste from distilleries. Well, Ben and Jerry's buys its milk only from Vermont family farms whose herds, free of growth hormone, range the fields. The ice cream made from that milk is first rate.

As for the mission, it's not only philanthropic, it's global. Ben and Jerry's has made a practice of working with the homeless and the unemployed. Some of their profits have gone to shelters and drug counselling centres. The company has been involved in the campaign to stop global deforestation.

Here's the point: Ben and Jerry's isn't the only super-premium ice-cream company in the world with a conscience. It *has,* however, been pre-eminent in its use of bucolic imagery. And, in a world that's been damaged by pollution and is as politically unstable as it has ever been, the imagery sells. So I have to think that what people are buying, in addition to the ice cream, is nostalgia—nostalgia for a past when milk was pure, cows were healthy, and life was guileless. I suspect our longing for a better time is not so far removed from Marie Antoinette's yearning for a better place. Maybe it's as close as we're ever going to get to Arcadia.

"Et in Arcadia ego"—that's the title Nicolas Poussin gave to his painting of a pastoral theme. Shepherds and shepherdesses gather around a tomb; one man kneels, and another points at the inscription on the stone. Everything that lives is subject to change and decay. Death is also in Arcadia. Now think of the saying figuratively, rather than literally. Nothing's ever perfect. Just when you're convinced you've got the world where you want it, something happens to change and upset the situation.

That was true in the long-running campaign to ban alcohol in the United States. The temperance movement, active through much of the nineteenth and into the twentieth centuries, and comprising several different groups with different strategies, was trying to bring about nothing less than a social revolution. The National Prohibition Party put forward temperance candidates for the presidency. The Anti-Saloon League practised the art of political lobbying. The Women's Christian Temperance Union (the WCTU) engaged in public education and developed a far-reaching and admirable social agenda. What brought the various groups together was their condemnation of "ardent spirits."

Milk and ice cream could provide alternatives. That was the movement's plan, at any rate. Members set out to build a world without alcohol, a world to which pastoral innocence could be restored. They persuaded soda fountains to eliminate drinks containing wine and liquor and start serving, along with egg flips, creams, and phosphates, ice-cream sodas and soda water flavoured with malted milk. This last, composed of malted cereals and dry evaporated milk, was a sort of early health food recommended for the care of babies and invalids. Malted milk became a key ingredient in a robust, "manly," nonalcoholic drink. And milkshakes—in the 1890s generally sweetened and flavoured milk, soda water, and sometimes a raw egg, vigorously shaken together—were also recommended as wholesome. The milk had to be very cold, and the ice cream, if it were added to the shake, slightly soft. Anyway, the new drinks took off, and everything seemed to be going smoothly in the campaign to displace alcohol.

Naturally, there were successes and setbacks. In Illinois in the nineteenth century, the husband of a warring couple who'd ended up in court was given a year's probation, provided he abstain from alcohol in favour of ice-cream sodas. In Pennsylvania, on the other hand, a wife was granted a divorce because her husband was doing precisely what the judge in Illinois had ordered: it seems he was spending *too* much time at the soda fountain, drinking sodas and neglecting the family poultry farm.

One of those unforeseen upsets was in the making. As towns passed laws against the abomination of drinking soda water on the Lord's Day (preachers delivered sermons against it), even ice cream could not save the ice-cream soda. It was banned in certain places. Then a band of druggists came forward with a solution. I say "band" because, as usual in the history of ice cream, there are several rival personalities to consider. Their solution was identical, however: just eliminate the soda water in the ice-cream soda, and what have you got?

THE CREAM OF LOVE.

CREAM OF LOVE

In 1881, in Two Rivers, Wisconsin, druggist Edward Berner responded to a customer's request for a soda by giving him ice cream with chocolate syrup instead. For the price of a nickel, anyone could buy one of his new "ice cream with syrup" concoctions. But only on Sundays. They involved far too much work for profit, too many dishes to buy, too much washing up. Then a little girl came in on a weekday and suggested a pretend Sunday. She got her wish. And the soda-less Sunday was born. Or did the little girl go into a drugstore called Giffy's, in Manitowac, Wisconsin, just six miles from Two Rivers? Only the location is changed; the story remains the same.

In 1892, in Ithaca, New York, druggist Chester C. Platt was serving plain vanilla ice cream to the minister of the local Unitarian church when he suddenly felt inspired. This is Platt's story. He poured cherry syrup over the ice cream and graced it with a maraschino cherry. His "cherry sunday" cost 10 cents. Ithaca was a busy place, it seems. In 1897, another drugstore laid claim to the invention of the name "sundae." The Red Cross Pharmacy was opposite the Ithaca Hotel. Because the hotel bar was closed on the Sabbath, customers crossed the road to the pharmacy for this socially acceptable treat with the new-fangled spelling.

Interesting that the town of Evanston, Illinois, was certain it was the first to come up with the term "ice cream sundae." Other variants—sundhi, sundaye— appeared in other locales, but they never had a chance. "Sundae" showed respect; it couldn't be confused with the Lord's day of rest. Although Evanston had been one of the first towns in the United States to ban ice-cream sodas, sundaes were another matter entirely, and the Evanston WCTU agreed. So Garwood's Drugstore was busy making and selling them. William C. Garwood was a pioneer of drive-in service. He nailed an electric bell to the trunk of a tree. When a carriage arrived on the premises, the driver pushed the bell. A clerk took the order and delivered the sundaes to customers, who were waiting in the shade of a tree.

Whatever the truth of all these competing claims, ice cream, shed of soda water, was fighting the good fight again. Soon, in New York City alone, soda fountains outnumbered saloons. When Prohibition arrived in 1920, many hotel bars turned into ice-cream parlours. Breweries became ice-cream factories. And the significance for hearth and home was not lost on ice-cream manufacturers. At one of their conventions, they inaugurated a rhyme sung to the tune of "Old Black Joe" that began, "Gone are the days when Father was a souse," and ended, "He's coming, he's coming; we can see him coming near—/ He brings a brick of ice cream home instead of beer."

The sundae remains the most memorable temperance dish of them all. It came with such accoutrements. There was the serving set itself: a metal dish, like a loving cup with two handles, a long spoon, both on a small tray. A glass alongside, preferably of cherry or claret phosphate, ice water, or ginger ale. (Well, under the circumstances, forget the *claret* phosphate, though it's a fact that during Prohibition some soda fountains cheated and continued to use alcohol in their drinks. And, when they were discovered, federal forces closed them down.) Then add any combo of marshmallows, marshmallow sauce, crushed pineapple, fruit syrups, roasted nuts, whipped cream, chocolate, coffee, caramel, cold toppings, hot toppings (just not hot enough to melt the ice cream)—sundaes were monuments to excess.

The *pièce de résistance* had to be three scoops of ice cream—chocolate, vanilla, and strawberry—over a split banana, seeds up, followed by strawberry syrup, chocolate syrup, pineapple topping, crushed nuts, and whipped cream, and finished with the flourish of a maraschino cherry or two plunked down on top: the classic banana split. It was placed in a glass dish shaped like a boat and specially designed to accommodate it. You'd think somebody would have condemned the extravagance. Gluttony, after all, is one of the Seven Deadly Sins. In fact, somebody did, and it proved to be a much larger issue than a sundae. It was an out-and-out attack on the ice-cream parlour itself as a den of iniquity.

In his article "Home Back," Francis M. McKee looks at Scotland in 1906, when the British Women's Temperance Association objected to Sunday openings—not of saloons (they weren't being considered) but of what were known to the Scots as "ice-cream shops." There had been stories of teenagers congregating in them, gambling in them, and using bad language in them. The *Glasgow Herald* reported police testimony to the effect that even prostitution could be traced back to girls' hanging about in ice-cream shops. They were worse than public houses, the newspaper reported. Lurking in the background was a distrust of foreigners and an anti-Catholic bias—Italians were running the establishments. Wisely, the owners courted the temperance movement to help calm the public. But it took two long years, in which they were constantly brought up on charges of gambling and selling liquor illegally.

Italians were involved in other businesses in Scotland. Why was ice cream targeted? Simply because it represented such luxury. According to McKee, ice cream was judged to be dangerous because it helped break down social inhibitions, adding "a new element of sexuality to public eating." When she's taken to a restaurant after a concert, even Anne of *Anne of Green Gables* tells Marilla there's something "dissipated" about sitting and eating ice cream in such a place. Late at night, to boot.

The very voluptuousness of the stuff, you see, set in motion a different way of dealing with the world. And that brings us back to the sundae. Actually, to the sundae of sundaes.

In 2004, the banana split celebrated its one-hundredth birthday, a veteran of the Prohibition wars. You can order one anywhere in Scotland and the rest of the British Isles. In the United States too, where, every year since 1997, the folks of Wilmington, Ohio, have been putting on a festival dedicated to it. They're convinced that the banana split was created by fellow citizen Frank Hazard. Meanwhile, the folks of Latrobe, Pennsylvania, where the local Elks Club sports a banana split on its official pin, are equally convinced that their own David Strickler was the originator. According to the good citizens of Latrobe, Strickler began slicing bananas and pumping syrup in his drugstore in 1904—three years before Hazard—inspired by work he'd seen a soda jerk do in Atlantic City, New Jersey. Today, you can indulge in a vertical version called the Rocket, in Elk Point, North Dakota; a tempura version in Coconut Grove, Florida; and an international take in Ko Samui, Thailand. You can't keep a good sundae down.

I think you could say that luxury has triumphed, although, as it turns out, there's still a price to be paid. All that fuss over ice cream and morality in recent history has left us—in English-speaking, Protestant parts of the world, at any rate—suffering from guilt, or believing we ought to be.

Maybe it's our legacy. We've been primed for it. The richer the ice cream, the more we describe it as "sinful," "decadent." We still experience ice cream as guilty pleasure, in other words. With its high fat, high sugar content, it's a frequent choice when bingeing. But I'm not talking about pathology here. Almost everyone feels guilt at giving in to excess and, indeed, revels in the pleasure of it.

The titillation can become really interesting when we pit one mythology of ice cream—its sinfulness—against another—its innocence. Cream against milk. Call it ice cream for adults, in which the dilemma is whether one guilty pleasure can meld into another, because, it appears, we *do* associate ice cream with sex.

In *Toast: The Story of a Boy's Hunger,* food writer Nigel Slater looks back at his childhood in terms of what he liked to eat and how he liked to eat it. In the section on ice cream, he's visiting the seaside with his parents, and he's having dinner with them. But his thoughts are fixed on the dessert that will surely come at the end of the meal. Three scoops, vanilla, strawberry, and chocolate, in a dish, with a wafer, fan-shaped if he's lucky, rectangular if he's not. He's as jumpy as a suitor and just as avid. When the ice cream *does* arrive, he savours each scoop individually, and, when the three are gone, as a final flourish he scrapes the dish, using his finger to catch whatever drops of ice cream might be lingering on the outside of it, even capturing what he refers to as "pearls of condensation." He's a boy, but he's also a man, and he writes about the experience with the awareness and sensuality of a man. The moral is: don't try to separate guilt from pleasure in the days of innocence or experience, whether it's ice cream or sex.

Consider the cow one last time. It's odd, when you think about it, that human beings drink its milk and eat ice cream containing its milk throughout their lives. Other creatures in the Great Chain of Being drink only the milk of their own mothers and only in infancy. (That is, if everything's operating as it should, with apologies to the cat and her saucer.) "In the beginning," as the Bible says, human beings did likewise. However, somewhere between 70,000 and 140,000 years ago, hunter-gatherers in Africa diverged from the common ancestral population. They moved into Eurasia, East Asia, Oceania, and ultimately the Americas and, in the process, became herders and farmers. Archaeological evidence suggests that goats and sheep were domesticated in Eurasia, for example, about a millennium before cattle, which became part of the farm some 8500 years ago.

So the herds were out there in the pen, producing milk every day of the year, and the idea must have struck *Homo sapiens:* Why not try it? The first man or woman who ventured to drink the fresh milk of a goat, sheep, or cow was a pioneer. "Ugh, hmm," he or she must have said (allow me a little poetic licence here), "tastes good!"

It was a textbook example of Darwin's survival of the fittest. The ability of the body to utilize milk protein for nourishment provided an edge for survival. So the lactase gene, which governs the body's ability to break down and absorb lactose, the sugar in milk, was passed on to successive generations. The enzyme lactase, which normally decreased after weaning, now continued in full force.

These biological changes happened, geneticists think, because of domestication and the beginnings of dairy farming. In both pre-recorded and recorded history, entire populations of adults as well as children had milk in their diet. Rock drawings from the Libyan Sahara show that dairying was taking place by about 4000 BC. A Sumerian fresco from 2500 BC shows cows being milked, the milk being put into jars, and the cream being poured into a churn, from which comes butter. By the time parts of the Old Testament were written, the Promised Land was being described as a land "flowing with milk and honey." Just not everyone's Promised Land. The matter isn't as clear-cut as I've made it sound.

Geneticists theorize that being lactose intolerant—unable to break down milk sugar—was the ancient, original state for *all* humans. It took eons for the pattern to change and, then, only for some. Peoples without a long, long history of herding animals—most Chinese, Japanese, Koreans, Jews in Israel and elsewhere, native Americans, and most Africans—can't digest milk beyond infancy without suffering the indignities of an attack on their digestive system. If they limit their intake to about a pint of milk a day, maybe they can handle it. That helps explain why, when ice cream was introduced to them in the twentieth century, the Chinese and Japanese were able to take delight in it (though the Chinese are still at the bottom of the list of global consumers). They simply kept their portions modest. As for South Asians, northern Europeans, Middle Easterners (Bedouins, Saudis, Yemenis), and the inhabitants of Central Asia, most of them can afford to indulge; they possess the gene.

Oh, the lactase gene—it sounds as though I'm talking about the philosopher's stone. But when it comes to eating ice cream, that gene is a treasure beyond compare. Without it, the blessings of milk surely will not flow.

Enter the lowly soybean to the rescue of those who are lactose intolerant and those who have a more complicated, life-threatening milk allergy. In some unlucky individuals, merely kissing someone who has drunk milk is enough to precipitate a severe allergic reaction to its protein. Well, the soybean is safe, it's nutritious, and it has its own mythology too. Long ago, the soybean was considered a sacred food in China, as sacred as milk, and it was part of everyone's fare, from the emperor to the peasant. It caught the attention of Western travellers, notably Domingo Fernández de Navarrete, a seventeenth-century Dominican friar. Navarrete described how soybeans were soaked in an alkaline solution, ground, brought to a boil, and, finally, filtered. The good friar referred to the resulting liquid as "milk." As did Li Yu-ying, who opened the world's first Western soy "dairy," near Paris, in 1910. Li Yu-ying's patent read: "vegetable milk and its derivatives."

But these days, soy is involved in a controversy similar to the one that swirls around Champagne and sparkling wine. It's been accused of appropriating what American dairy producers have claimed is "milk's good name." What they're suggesting is that the bean, lodged in the dairy aisle of most modern supermarkets, is usurping the cow.

So how do the blessings of the soybean flow for those of us who have the lactase gene and can choose either way? Recently, I bought some soy ice cream. Except it didn't refer to itself as "ice cream"; the label read "frozen dessert." I tried an informal, very informal, blind test with a friend.

"Close your eyes," I told her, "and I'll hand you a spoon with either ice cream or the soy on it. You tell me which you prefer." I gave her spoon No. 1 and waited for her response.

"Mmm." She licked her lips. "Mmm, that's good."

I gave her spoon No. 2. In went the spoon, and there was a long pause.

"That's go-o-o-d too," she said, "but not as good as the first one. This is good, but it's grainy."

"Which is which?"

She didn't hesitate. "The first one's ice cream," she said.

She was right, of course. I tried the soy myself and agreed with her. Its texture was grainy, and, as it melted, it left a taste that I didn't like on my tongue, just before the flavour of chocolate took over and reassured me.

All my little test proves, of course, is that we're habituated to tastes and textures. We think ice cream should be smooth if we've grown up with it smooth, should taste one way and not another.

It so happens I bought the soy product in a health food store. It took the health food movement to make soy sexy to the West. Since the 1960s, soy farmers and manufacturers have been promoting their product, fortified with calcium and vitamins (particularly B_{12}), as healthier than you know what. Vegetarians depend on soy. Think of bean curd, tofu, tempeh, miso, soy sauce, so central to their diet. As for soy ice cream—okay, I admit, I find it awkward to refer to it as "soy frozen dessert"—it has also been embraced wholeheartedly by the counter-culture.

In an interesting vignette in the *San Francisco Chronicle* in December 2003, Stephen Gaskin, the founder of the Farm, once the largest hippie commune in the United States, is eating lunch at home in Tennessee. It consists of stir-fried vegetables and a bowl of soy ice cream. (Well, *you* decide what to call it.) During its heyday, the Farm used to produce its own soy products, and, in the lingo of the sixties, the bean was part of an "alternative lifestyle." When he's finished his meal, Gaskin settles down to make a prophecy: as retirees, former residents of the Farm will return to the idea of collectivity. He's busy planning a retirement village in place of the commune that collapsed in the 1980s, but with the same values. Drugs will be a matter of personal choice. Everyone will build his or her own house. And Gaskin will be responsible for providing a community centre, clinic, kitchen, laundromat, and media room, complete with computers and access to the internet. In such a setting, it could be argued that a "soy frozen dessert" represents a protest against milk drinkers and ice-cream eaters of the mainstream.

The same could also be said of hemp "ice cream," which has begun showing up at green festivals in Britain and North America and is made from hemp seeds crushed in water. (It contains no dairy and no saturated fats, and there's a slightly nutty aftertaste.) And it worries

AN INQUIRY
INTO THE NATURE
OF ICE CREAM

What is the nature of ice cream? Here are two ways to come at it: as intentional discovery or accidental find. Immediately, worlds that are poles apart are revealed. For example, Martha Washington, wife of George (who loved ice cream), is supposed to have left a bowl of sweetened cream out on their back doorstep. Overnight, the temperature dropped, and the cream congealed. The next morning Mrs. Washington tasted what she found, loved it, and that's how ice cream was born. This tale is so simple and believable, it appears to render further inquiry unnecessary.

But what if you asked instead what changes were occurring in Martha's bowl of cream that night? What if you set out to understand the process empirically? Story would give way to test, accident to intention, and another kind of truth would be revealed. Still, you don't have to sacrifice one truth for another. Let them keep company, I say, and that's what I'm going to do here: provide some stories, along with a little history and research, to get at the essence of ice cream. You can take the stories with a grain of salt. Literally, as well as figuratively.

As Mark Kurlansky points out in his book *Salt: A World History,* this compound is crucial: our bodies need salt to survive. It's powerful: salt seasons and preserves our food. It's multifaceted: the everyday uses of salt are mind-boggling. It seasons, removes rust, seals cracks, puts out grease fires, kills poison ivy, removes spots on clothes, keeps cut flowers fresh, makes candles dripless, cleans bamboo furniture, treats sore throats, sprains, and earaches, stiffens white organdy—and has a hand in freezing ice cream. That's just part of the list that Kurlansky provides in his book. But he merely mentions the importance of salt to ice cream without going into any detail. And it's the detail that is truly remarkable. Thanks to salt, ice cream exists, a triumph of the intellect, the result of experiments to evolve the science of freezing in centuries past.

"The Producing of Cold is a thing very worthy of the Inquisition," Sir Francis Bacon observed in the seventeenth century. In his posthumously published *Sylva Sylvarum,* or "A Natural History," he wrote, "Whosoever will be an enquirer into Nature let him resort to a conservatory of Snow or Ice"—have an ice house, in other words, for experiments. Bacon was interested in making artificial ice. He wrote down freezing mixtures that he knew his contemporaries were using. And he studied the effects of cold on nature.

It's ironic that it was cold, as only Mother Nature could produce, that was blamed for his death. In 1626, the story goes, when he was out on Highgate Hill, taking the air with a friend, he alighted from his coach, wondering "why flesh might not be preserved in snow as in Salt." (There's that salt again.) Bacon managed to procure a chicken from an old woman living at the bottom of the hill and began stuffing it with snow to determine how long it would take to freeze. That's how, so it was said, he caught a chill and died from bronchial pneumonia ten days later, a champion to the end of the experimental method he believed would explain creation.

It has to be noted that Bacon's idea of cold was different from ours. For him, it was not the absence of heat.

Cold was an entity, with its own properties and secrets, so the quest was to discover them and understand the entity in and of itself. But Bacon also observed that when common salt was added to water, it "intensified" (his word) the cold. We would say that salt acts endothermically—that is, it absorbs heat—and from that understanding, so much frozen pleasure has ensued.

"Salting something away"; "pillar of salt," as in "turned into." I was running through associations that could be made with the word. "Salt lick," what cattle need; "the salt mines," as in "I've been working in." I'd gone to the local variety story, put coins in the slot of the ice machine and retrieved a large plastic bag of ice cubes. I'd also picked up a couple of boxes of table salt. I was on my way to make ice cream with my friend Michèle. At that moment, Francis Bacon caught me dead to rights: "Here, therefore, the first distemper of learning, when men study words and not matter."

Okay, I admit that science worries me. I don't take to it easily, preferring to deal with the world through words. But you can't make ice cream without dealing with matter, and you can't handle matter without a scientific frame of mind. Happily, the science was done long ago by those gifted in that regard. Let me supply a summary.

A verse in a fourth-century Indian poem called *Pancatantra* attests that only by using salt can water be made very cold. As for freezing it, in the thirteenth century an Arab historian of medicine, Ibn Abu Usaybi'a, gave directions for making artificial ice—basically, by mixing cold water and saltpetre (a form of sodium nitrate or potassium nitrate). The Arabs probably learned the method from the Chinese, who also invented gunpowder (saltpetre, sulphur, and carbon). And who knows exactly when the Chinese began thinking about making ice? According to Kurlansky, Chinese historians are convinced that crystals of sodium chloride—common salt—were being collected from Lake Yuncheng, in the northern part of the country, by 6000 BC. In the summer, the lake was dry, and the salt could be harvested. The first written account of boiling sea water to collect salt crystals dates from 800 BC and claims that the enterprise began during the Xia dynasty, a millennium earlier. Making sea salt finally reached the West through the Romans, who, in all likelihood, learned the method from the Arabs.

There have always been different kinds of salt in the world. In the story of ice cream, experiments using saltpetre, or "nitre," as it was also known, prove a fascinating chapter.

A certain Dr. Zimara of Padua University was the first European to declare in writing that saltpetre could help chill as well as explode. That was in 1530. In 1550, Blas Villafranca, a Spanish doctor, instructed readers how to cool wine and water with saltpetre. In 1559, in his book *Occulta Naturae Miracula (The Secret Miracles of Nature)*, the Dutch physician Levinus Lemnius explained that wine could be preserved by taking it out of the cask, pouring it into pots, and immersing the pots in a container of cold water. Then, he advised, saltpetre should be added to the container of water, "and it will so cool the wine that your teeth can hardly endure it."

This may be the first recorded description of what we now refer to as an "ice-cream headache," which is caused by blood vessels dilating for fifteen or twenty seconds when cold hits nerves in the roof of your mouth. Or it could simply be the impact of cold on sensitive teeth. But Lemnius was convinced that saltpetre, "which makes such a noise in Guns," was the *agent provocateur*. (By the way, if you want to avoid such a headache, don't eat or drink

METHODUS REFRIGERANDI EX VOCATO SALENITIO VINUM AQUAMQUE
(A DEVICE FOR COOLING WINE AND WATER)
BLAS VILLAFRANCA, 1550. A FLASK IS TURNED BY HAND
IN A TUB OF SNOW AND SALTPETRE.

anything cold too quickly and keep it away from the roof of your mouth.)

Finally, in 1589, Giambattista Della Porta, a mathematician and "natural philosopher" like Francis Bacon, advised shaking together a bowl of saltpetre and snow to produce a "mighty cold," discovering, it seems, that agitating the "cooling agents" could double the fun by increasing the effect.

These are only some of the Renaissance men who helped deliver artificial ice to a world that was still relying on stockpiles from nature. Ice was far too expensive to manufacture for general use. But the Europeans were gradually learning how water reacted when salt was added to it and how salt could chill and, ultimately, freeze other liquids, beginning with wine.

There was an unexpected food dividend to their work, even though it didn't mean as much to them. According to one of his contemporaries, by the time he died in 1587, Francesco I, grand duke of Tuscany, was pouring boiling white-grape must—unfermented new wine—over iced milk. There's also a story that he combined frozen milk, egg yolk, and malmsey—a strong sweet wine—to make a drink. If the story is to be believed, he was in his laboratory in the Palazzo Vecchio late into the midnight hours, inventing libations to please himself, clocking off miles on the road to ice cream. Francesco was only one of many. You can imagine the scholars in their studies, like Marlowe's Dr. Faustus, huddling over texts and refining formulae; the scientists in their laboratories, like Paracelsus, measuring into flasks, pots, and brass basins as they tried to unlock the secrets of the universe—to understand cold, at any rate. Soon they were experimenting with rudimentary air conditioning.

Let's acknowledge that they were "worth their salt." If you knew something about freezing various liquids and you published your results (which they did), you made it possible for others to come along later and create all kinds of frozen confections. And, with a certain amount of stirring and shaking going on, the idea might have been planted for an early ice-cream maker: the *sorbetière* (or *sarbotière*), a lidded pot with a handle attached to the lid, which Benjamin Franklin is believed to have brought home with him from Europe, or the pot-freezer, which George Washington, among others, used at home (a room-by-room inventory of Washington's possessions done after his death lists two pewter and eight tin ice-cream pots at Mount Vernon). It didn't matter that pot-freezing was such a time-consuming process, inelegant and primitive. What mattered was that science had paved the way. Though the two presidents surely never did any such thing themselves, it's irresistible to picture them, spatula in hand, scraping the ice-cream base off the walls of the pot and rotating or shaking the pot in a large pan of ice and salt.

After a while—four centuries, in fact—saltpetre fell out of favour. It contained too many impurities, and people simply didn't like its connection to gunpowder. Common salt prevailed. However, Francis Bacon, for one, in his *Novum Organum* of 1620, realized that common salt contributed to a much more complicated, overlapping physics and chemistry of freezing: "Nitre or salt when added to snow or ice intensifies the cold of the latter, the nitre by adding its own cold, but the salt by supplying activity to the cold of the snow." With that said, I'm going to attempt to describe (I use the word *attempt* because it's a very complicated business) a more up-to-date version of what happens inside an ice-cream machine.

The machine in question, my friend Michèle's, uses ordinary table salt and ice cubes. That's why I took two boxes to her house, along with a bag of artificial ice cubes. Now you know.

We were standing in Michèle's kitchen, contemplating her electric ice-cream maker. "My mother bought me this one as a present," Michèle said. "I wouldn't be tackling homemade ice cream without it."

We had decided on chocolate ice cream. Michèle was making it, and I was watching, and we were right at a critical juncture. She was about to put the custard base—among other ingredients, sugar syrup, cocoa powder, egg yolks, milk, cream, vanilla extract, and bittersweet chocolate, the Belgian kind—into the maker. To cool it down after cooking it, she'd placed the custard in her freezer. "I've probably chilled the custard too fast," she said. "It's best if it sits for several hours. If it were winter, I'd just stick it outside." She poured the velvety, densely brown, almost-black liquid base into the metal canister, put its lid on, and inserted the canister into the machine. In went the dasher, or paddle, after it. "Making ice cream is basically like churning butter," she said and began layering ice and salt around the outside of the canister. A layer of salt, a layer of ice, repeated all the way to the top. Then she flipped the switch.

At the heart of the noise that erupted inside the ice-cream maker (it's an old machine), energy began to fly in a purposeful direction. Well, not "fly" exactly, but the equilibrium was definitely and deliberately upset. Adding salt lowered the temperature inside the machine. It also caused the ice to melt, exactly as it does on sidewalks in winter. If you're scratching your head right now, just remember that heat and temperature are not the same thing. The chemical term for what occurs is "freezing point depression." As the salt dissolved in the water from the ice it was melting, it formed a concentrated brine solution on the surface of the ice cubes, and that solution has a very low freezing point. More and more ice melted, trying to achieve equilibrium between solid and liquid.

This is where the endothermism comes in. The brine solution adsorbed—yes, that's *ad*sorbed—heat from the contents in the canister, meaning it gathered heat in a condensed layer on the ice cubes' surface. So Michèle had to keep adding more salt and ice because ice cream requires a temperature lower than the freezing point of water—32°F, or 0°C—to freeze.

Let me express it another way. Within the ice-cream maker, water molecules dispensed energy in the form of heat. The heat broke up the salt crystals into electrically charged positive and negative ions. The ions, in turn, attracted the water molecules, leaving fewer to combine with the ice. Thus the normal exchange of energy between water and ice was disturbed; the water lost heat, and the temperature dropped. The exchange of energy in this play of molecules and ions constantly moving and changing was poetry as much as science in motion.

And speaking of motion, Michèle was busy tossing ice cubes and salt into the machine. "Ooh, it's cold! I have to do it with my hands. It's the only way to get the cubes in." Too little salt and the ice cream wouldn't freeze completely. Too *much* salt and the ice cream would get too hard, too fast. But the ratio was just right. Round and round the dasher went until, gradually, the burgeoning ice cream began to form its own pure ice crystals, and the base stiffened. That's when the machine had finished its work, and Michèle switched it off. If the dasher had churned any longer, butter particles would have formed, and the ice cream would have curdled.

"Okay, I'm taking the dasher out." Michèle handed it to me. Licking it was a revelation. The ice cream coating the dasher was soft, with an intensely brooding, almost smoky, dangerous flavour. "I think I'd call this Chocolate Heart Attack!" Michèle laughed as she ladled the soft chocolate ice cream into a plastic container. In the final stage, it would sit in the freezer to harden, or "ripen" or "season" as though it were a sultry fruit.

But not for long. The eating would take place sooner rather than later, because experience dictates that ice cream is at its best just after it's been made, when it seems, in Alexander Pope's words, "to walk on wings, / and tread in air." Ice cream falls to Earth—deteriorates, that is, in quality, texture, and taste—every time it is taken out of the freezer. It becomes less than the perfection it is.

Here are a few facts. Some of the liquid in ice cream always remains unfrozen. You wouldn't be able to scoop it if it was solid through and through. Ice cream is only ever a partly frozen foam, in which ice crystals and fat globules "tread" on air bubbles. The air, beaten in by the dasher, holds the fat and ice in suspension. Fat globules carry flavour, create a smoother texture, and also help keep small ice crystals apart, preventing them from fusing and forming larger crystals.

Avoiding a rock-solid confection was a major challenge in the making of early ice creams. In his recipe from 1696 for Orange Flower Snow—cream, powdered sugar, and fresh or candied petals of orange flowers—François Pierre La Varenne recommended that, during the freezing process, the mixture be shaken several times so that it wouldn't freeze solid. It was a case of ice crystals left pretty much to their own devices; there wasn't enough fat in the recipe to stop them from running wild. The proper ratio of fat to air to ice was as yet unknown.

These days, there can be such a thing as getting too much air. In ice-cream making, a certain amount is necessary and is defined as "overrun." Air increases the volume in homemade ice cream by about a third. But commercial ice creams can *double* in volume through the introduction of compressed air during churning—just scraping past the letter of the law, since percentages of overrun are now regulated. For example, the FDA in the United States, Agriculture Canada, and the Food Standards Agency in Britain all permit 100 percent overrun, resulting in an ice cream that is 50 percent air.

But that's small consolation to some. James Logue, who was a philosopher at Oxford University and a Fellow of Somerville College, told me this story.

Somerville is well known as the college where Margaret Thatcher was an undergraduate. She used to like to boast later in life that she was the only prominent British politician with a science degree, and it's true that she did a degree in chemistry at the college. But the only scientific work she's known to have done, shortly after graduating, was to spend eighteen months or so discovering methods of injecting air into ice cream. I believe she managed to get it to the point where 35 percent was water, 15 percent other products, none of them dairy. And 50 percent was air. [Think of the profit! Think of the spin!]

The ice cream was marketed and sold on the basis that it was incredibly light and fluffy. And it seems to me so wonderfully appropriate for a prime minister who's later going to privatize the nation's assets and sell them back to the people who already own them to start out her career by taking the bounty of nature and somehow selling it back to people who had it for free.

Logue had a point. The fact is, cheaper ice cream contains more air than fat. In premium and superpremium ice creams the opposite is true: there's more fat than air. In homemade ice cream, the fat comes from milk and cream, "the bounty of nature."

At this very moment, in my freezer, I happen to have a "frozen dessert." I bring the carton out and read the ingredients: maltodextrin, polydextrose, sorbitol, glycerine, cellulose gel, cellulose gum, mono- and diglycerides, guar gum, carob bean gum, carrageenan, aspartame (containing phenylalanine), and partame (containing phenylalanine and acesulfamen). That's just a partial accounting of what lies beneath the cardboard cover. It will teach me to pay more attention to the label before I buy, though I'd need a food chemist standing by to interpret.

Some of the words are in the dictionary. Turns out they're thickening agents, sweeteners (did I neglect to mention this is a low-fat, sugarless frozen dessert?), stabilizers, emulsifiers. Once, gelatin was the stabilizer of choice. Now a combination of plant materials that come from beans, red algae, seaweed, and brown kelp helps to keep the ice cream firm. In the past, egg yolks were nature's emulsifiers. Today, along with a little dried egg yolk, mono- and diglycerides from vegetable or animal fats and oils keep the ice cream smooth.

But where are the milk and cream? Apparently, these luxuries have been replaced by "milk ingredients" and "modified milk ingredients." Too much of the laboratory about this one, I realize, too much doctoring and processing.

But I'm protesting after the fact. I don't need to watch my weight, and yet I bought this product. Ever heard the term "conspicuous consumption"? It was coined in 1902 by the American economist Thorstein Veblen to describe a defining characteristic of the leisure class: their conspicuous consumption of the best society had to offer and that they could afford. Only the richest food and drink need apply. Well, this frozen concoction caters to a sort of inverse conspicuous consumption, still with pretensions. Everybody wants to believe that they belong, if not to a leisure class, then certainly to an upwardly mobile one. In Veblen's day, portliness of the body could be regarded as a sign of wealth. But now that thin is fashionable and unsightly creases or bulges must never appear, food has trimmed down too. A "frozen dessert" is created so that everybody can eat ice cream—or rather, its counterfeit—and not pay the price of added pounds. All through chemistry.

You're probably going to counter: "Lots of commercial ice creams are rich in fat—milk and cream fat, butterfat. They're lavish, extravagant, advertising that they contain no artificial flavours or colours, that they're not artificially stabilized and emulsified—or very little. They crow about it. And they're just as fashionable, maybe more." I'd argue that's unalloyed Veblen. People can go off their diet and indulge themselves once in a while. Ice cream becomes a luxurious, pricey treat again.

Of course, our desires are manipulated by clever marketing. Remember the Eskimo Pie? It was the inspiration of a candy-store proprietor, Christian Nelson, in Onawa, Iowa. In 1919, Nelson realized that people would flock to buy a chocolate-covered vanilla ice-cream bar. By 1921, he'd figured out how to make the chocolate cling (he used cocoa butter), had entered into joint partnership with an ice-cream company, and had sold out the bars they made one hot summer in Des Moines. A year later, he was selling a million pies a day.

That's ancient history. In 1999, the Eskimo Pie was deep in the doldrums when a Canadian company, CoolBrands, acquired the brand. First, it smartened up the packaging, making the new Eskimo Pie attractive to the eye, irresistible to buy. Simple enough. Then the company began to capitalize on the apparent contradiction between eating ice cream and wanting to be slim.

It seems CoolBrands entered the more complicated world of Veblen, putting on the market something it called the Slender Pie, which is more expensive than the Eskimo Pie, double the price for a six-pack. As Veblen declared in his essay "Conspicuous Consumption": "If these articles of consumption are costly, they are felt to be noble and honorific." Today, the Slender Pie, made from a low-calorie sweetener, and 98 percent fat free, outsells the original. And here's the kicker. When CoolBrands licensed the Weight Watchers Smart Ones brand, it manufactured an ice-cream sandwich that was more than

100 percent larger than its predecessor under the diet plan. How was size increased without violating the point system of Weight Watchers? According to the candid admission of the president and co-CEO of CoolBrands: "Air."

I find myself wondering what Francis Bacon and company back in the sixteenth and seventeenth centuries would make of our brave new world of frozen desserts and designer ice creams: low cholesterol, low carb, vegetarian, non-dairy kosher, frozen yogurt for the conscientiously healthy, and tofu-based and bean-curd-based for the lactose intolerant. What you see isn't all you get. There's the invisible presence of inert fillers and bulking agents to shape a comely scoop. Shelf life is built in with additives, so the product can last for weeks or months in the freezer. As Shakespeare put it, "All that glisters isn't gold." Bacon, for his part, noted that it's wise to have "the power to feign, if there be no remedy."

As for Veblen's ideal of extravagance, I can't resist offering you this imagined scene of sumptuous dining at the end of the nineteenth century. The meal includes a soup course, a fish course, an entrée, and a relevé—that is, a roast with vegetables. (That there were multiple courses is no surprise to you.) The meal is also punctuated by ice cream. Perhaps a slushy punch in a tall glass before the soup, although punch began to go out of fashion in Victorian times. Or a sorbet, as recommended in Mrs. A. B. Marshall's *Book of Ices,* made with lemons, wine, or spirits, to refresh the palate. Mrs. Marshall suggests serving the sorbets after the soup and preceding the serving of the "joint" or roast. They should be presented, she says, "in glasses or fancy cups, and generally just enough frozen to be piled up in the glass, or they may be moulded in little shapes and served with or without fruit." As the meal draws to a close, the final course is introduced, with its sweet and savoury ices, incorporating asparagus, spinach, cucumbers, as you please.

Here's the recipe for a satisfying sweet at the end of the meal, Mrs. Marshall's version of chocolate ice cream.

....

MRS. A. B. MARSHALL'S CHOCOLATE CREAM ICE

For custard:

1 pint of cream

1/4 pound of castor sugar

8 egg yolks

Put the cream in a pan over the fire, and let it come to the boil, and then pour it on to the sugar and yolks in a basin and mix well. Return it to the pan and keep it stirred over the fire till it thickens and clings well to the spoon, but do not let it boil; then pass it through a tammy or hair sieve, or strainer. Let it cool; add vanilla or other flavour, and freeze. When partly frozen, half a pint of whipped cream slightly sweetened may be added to each pint of custard.

For cream ice:

4 ounces of semisweet chocolate
1/2 cup plus 2 Tb milk or cold water
2 1/2 cups custard or cream

Cut a quarter of a pound of vanilla chocolate very fine, and put it in a quarter of a pint of milk or cold water on the stove to cook till quite dissolved; then add this to 1 pint of custard or 1 pint of sweetened cream (sweetened with a quarter of a pound of castor sugar). Freeze and mould or serve in glasses.

....

When Michèle's homemade chocolate ice cream reached the table the day of its making, everyone agreed that it was worthy of the most discriminating appreciation. And it was served with the style and reverence it deserved: Michèle scooped it into glass dishes from the 1930s, green, pink, and delicate. Ice cream *is* delicate. It must remain frozen to be at its best.

Fluctuations in temperature cause thawing and refreezing. New ice crystals form. Everyone has had the experience of bringing home ice cream only to find it's a sorry mess of crystals, sometimes even solid ice. Who knows how often it has partly thawed and been refrozen? And the damage accumulates. Too much fluctuation in temperature and the ice cream will go into something known as heat shock. It is destabilized. Its smoothness and creaminess are lost, and its deterioration is complete.

Don't get me wrong. I'm not arguing for artificial stabilizers. I'm merely pointing out that ice cream requires more sensitive handling than, say, a package of frozen peas. When it's homemade, it begins to go into a decline within twenty-four hours.

"What I've noticed about homemade ice cream is that it melts very quickly," Michèle said. Ah, but this was the moment when we *wanted* it to melt, at room temperature, so we could see what was happening in the glass dishes. All ice cream collapses when it melts—the correct term is "melt-down"—but in commercial varieties, of course, the event is artificially delayed. There was something wonderfully reassuring about the melt-down of Michèle's homemade chocolate ice cream. It pooled. It melted. And as it melted, the fragrance of real Belgian chocolate wafted up from the spoon. Just as licking it off the dasher had been, eating it now was a deeply sensuous experience. When ice cream is soft or melting, it tastes sublime—I would claim it can even be inhaled.

In his own private experiment, Raymond Sokolov, a food writer and the former food editor of the *New York Times,* put this theory to the test. He sampled containers of chocolate and vanilla taken directly from his freezer, from his refrigerator, and from his kitchen table, where he placed two of the containers to warm up. He concluded, "The more solid, the less dramatic the taste," and that "cold tends to reduce the intensity of flavour."

What enchants me about Sokolov's experiment is the experience that put it in his mind in the first place. While he was in Martinique in 1972, he came across a woman in the main square of Fort-de-France standing in the sun, selling ice cream from a container set in a tub of ice. She was almost out of ice cream because it was late in the day, and what was left was very soft. Sokolov bought two scoops of banana, "still cold enough to hold their shape," and ate them with a plastic spoon. He still remembers that banana ice cream warmed by the sun. The thing itself is not simply how it's explained but also how it's experienced. And sometimes they're part of the same package. Narrative is as much a part of the nature of ice cream as science is.

Right now, to the left of my computer, there's a dish on my desk, in which sits a portion of the "frozen dessert" I told you about earlier. It's taking a long, long time to melt. It hasn't collapsed yet, but there's a very modest thaw at the edges. I'm lifting a spoonful to my mouth ... in it goes ... and it deposits a dull, synthetic, metallic taste on my tongue. If the so-called dessert hadn't been sitting out while I've been writing, if it weren't melting in its own inhibited way, the chemistry, the *deus ex machina*, might have escaped notice. What remains will simply dwindle away into an insignificant puddle. All the air pumped into it has flown away.

Fact: "Economy" ice cream relies on the maximum amount of emulsifiers and stabilizers to make it smooth, give it "chew-resistance," and protect it against heat shock.

Fact: Sugar contributes body to ice cream, but, by increasing the density of the base, it also lowers the freezing point. When ice crystals begin to form, the sugar—dissolved in eggs or milk or cream—becomes even more concentrated, and the freezing point is lowered further still. This process continues until the sugar concentration is so high and the freezing point so low there will always be some liquid in the ice cream.

Fact: There are national preferences in ice cream. Rich, lush, smooth—French. Sweet, rich, soft—American. Dense, colder, milkier—Italian. Argentineans like their gelato less creamy than the Italians. Filipinos bump up American ice cream with indigenous flavours such as purple yam and coconut. Mexicans enjoy rice-flavoured ice cream on a stick.

Maybe that's what makes the hunt for the most memorable ice cream so determined. It's really a search for the continuation of a long, differentiated history of making, selling, and eating. To realize what the hunt entails, you just have to ask a committed ice-cream connoisseur like James Logue, who was dauntless in his pursuit of the best. So I did.

"The absolute best ice cream is served in little paper cups and eaten with plastic spoons," he told me. "You can always tell you're somewhere serious when you get it served that way."

He meant, I think, that attention should be focused on the quality of the ice cream, not on presentation. Behind his remark is a legacy of small cafés and individual entrepreneurs, including the confectioner Philip Lenzi, who advertised his jams, jellies, pastries, sugar plums, and ice cream in New York City in 1774. In May 1777, while the British Army was occupying the city, Lenzi, uncertain about his fate, moved from Dock Street to Hanover Square. Nevertheless, he advertised his move and let it be known in the New York *Gazette* that he would carry on his business come what may.

"I'm prepared to fight my way down through Manhattan in a blizzard, in January, to buy the best ice cream and then eat it in the street," James Logue admitted. "About a dozen years ago, I was informed there was a little place down in lower Manhattan—my informant wasn't quite sure where or what it was called, but said a guy named Steve worked there. The north winds were whipping down the avenues, and people were talking about life-threatening cold. I remember spending hours wandering around and being delighted when I finally found it."

"Did it fulfill expectations?" I wanted to know.

"It fulfilled expectations, as they were at that stage. But that was before I discovered Bertillon in Paris or Vivoli in Florence and learned what really good ice cream is like."

Bertillon, on the Ile Saint Louis, offers a tiny scoop, no more than two tablespoons of each concentrated *parfum,* as the establishment puts it. Now that's an interesting word for flavour. At Bertillon you will find lemon, melon, raspberry, chocolate, pear, cinnamon, and over fifty more *parfums*.

"Bertillon is principally a take-away," James Logue said. "You queue up, get served, and then walk in one of the most beautiful parts of Paris"—through streets lined with seventeenth-century houses—"and that's bound to add to the experience."

The seventeenth century was an auspicious century in the history of French ice cream. In 1686, a Sicilian named Francesco Procopio dei Coltelli opened a legendary establishment in Paris. (You'll encounter his name more than once in this book.) He professed to be not only a *limonadier* (a maker of lemonade), a *liquoriste,* and a distiller but also an apothecary. And that has given rise to an image of Procopio sitting in his laboratory, testing and tasting, a little alcohol here, a little fruit syrup there, a little seed or flower essence here and there, creating exquisite and intense flavours. Procopio was reputed to be the man who introduced the eating of ices to ordinary Parisians. True or not, he set the standard for all those who enter the French ice-cream trade.

"On the other hand," James continued, "Vivoli has the look of an old-fashioned ice-cream parlour, with wooden flooring. It's just off the Piazza Santa Croce in Florence."

"The birthplace of Dante Alighieri, the poet of *The Divine Comedy*," I said.

"Yes. I happened to visit Vivoli recently, and I was thinking about ice cream in a very Dantesque way."

"What do you mean?"

"It struck me that there's an eschatology to ice cream. You take in the substance, and you enjoy the heavenly taste. But at the same time, you have this sense that perhaps there's something sinful about encountering such very, very intense flavours. The inner circles of Dante's Hell are made of ice, not fire." (Here a small, dry chuckle.)

In seventeenth-century Florence, doctor and poet Francesco Redi was involved in a similar kind of game.

He was writing *Arianna Infirma* (Ariadne Ailing), and he employed his own eschatology of ice cream. Though he didn't complete the poem before he died in 1698, the fragments that remain contain not only an exuberant description of eating a *sorbetto*—"Oh how it crackles between the teeth and dissolves"—but also an urging of fellow physicians to prescribe ices for their patients. According to Redi, if they did, hospitals would close, and that would leave Charon, the ferryman in Hell, "slumbering on his barque on the shore of Acheron." In other words, eating ice cream could help keep patients alive, healthy, and *out* of Hell.

(Incidentally, Redi was physician to the grand duke of Tuscany, in the line of succession from Francesco I—he of the recipes for milk and malmsey.)

Sure, it's an exaggeration to read heaven and hell into the experience of eating ice cream, whether your model is Dante or a Roman myth. But as James Logue also told me: "It's a tribute to how potent the experience of eating ice cream is that we feel the necessity to provide a mythology for it." James spoke about ice cream as others speak about wine, keenly savouring quality where he found it. He had a philosophical case to make, since that was his profession, about the distinction between higher and

SCACCHI'S FRIGIDARIUM, 1622
THE JAR (E) IS FILLED WITH SNOW AND PLACED INTO THE CONTAINER (A),
WHERE THE LID IS MARKED (B). THE BOTTLE (F), CONTAINING WINE OR
WATER, IS PLACED IN ONE OF THE OPENINGS ON EITHER SIDE (C).

lower pleasures that goes all the way back to Aristotle. "I think the importance of ice cream is that it calls into question this easy distinction," he said. "If we were simply wallowing in a lower pleasure, we wouldn't be motivated to come up with images and stories about it."

Caveat: Only the best and most brilliant ice cream can inspire such an imaginative response. Or at least the attempt at one. I know because I found out for myself.

In Montreal, in May 2001, I arrived at the restaurant Toqué in the quiet of an early afternoon before the rush of dinnertime preparation had begun. I followed Normand Laprise, the owner and chef, back to his kitchen. Depending on his inclination and what's fresh that day, that season, Monsieur Laprise makes his own ice cream from milk, cream, sugar, and egg yolks (a classic French ice cream); his own sorbet from fresh fruit pulp; and his own ice milk from just milk, sugar, spices and herbs (maybe basil, coriander, or tarragon, among many possibilities). As part of a meal in his restaurant, these ices run the gamut. They're an apéritif; they cleanse the palate between courses; they're a dessert. Normand Laprise is an artist who is following in the tradition of grand dining.

"I have the control," he said in his heavily accented English. "I know where is the fruit. There's no chemical inside. Sometimes people put a lot of preservatives and colouring, and, when a sorbet's pink or red, it's food colouring. I prefer to go with the real food produce." One winter, he had an affair with a truffle. First, he stored it with eggs in a large jar. Then, when the eggs had taken on the truffle flavour, he made a custard base with the yolks, adding a slice of truffle when the base was placed in the ice-cream machine to be churned. Flecks of black appeared embedded in a fragrant, sweet, and earthy surprise. "I put it in a bowl with a little bit of caramelized sugar on the top." He smiled. "It's all about playing with expectations." The aroma preceded the truffle ice cream into the restaurant.

We stepped into his small, narrow dessert kitchen, and Monsieur Laprise led me to a counter. To the right of us was the gleaming metal ice-cream machine from Switzerland. To the left, below the counter, the small refrigerator where he kept each individual base. Today's: clove; rhubarb; strawberry—"very light," he said; anise; blueberry. One by one, he took them out and offered me samples in little paper cups. Some of them he gave a spin in the Swiss machine; they were ready in two minutes. Each of them painted a picture. It was like eating in technicolour, more real than real, and I tried and failed to describe them to myself. The anise ice milk, which tasted like licorice, naturally, reminded me of school days gone by ... lame. Rhubarb, fresh that day from rural Quebec, took me out into the countryside ... predictable. The flavours kept coming. Clove ... creamy, spicy, concentrated. Strawberry ... vivid, intense, bright ... mmm, wow, fantastic! I began to sound silly to myself as I tried to capture so much sensation. Not so experienced in this arena of connoisseurship as James Logue or Francesco Redi, out loud I muttered simply, "Delicious!"

That evening, I had dinner at Toqué. As a finish to a memorable meal, I ordered the dessert to end all desserts: one slice of pound cake caramelized in rosemary oil and topped with strawberry and rhubarb sorbet *à la minute*.

"When you ask for your sorbet, my ice-cream machine can make everything *à la minute*," Chef Normand had advised me, "fresh, smooth, and not too cold." I prepared myself for what was to come, let my senses take over, and rejoiced in the moment.

One of the most famous works on gastronomy was published in Paris in 1825. It bore the extravagant title *Physiologie du goût, ou Méditations de gastronomie transcendante: ouvrage théorique, historique et à l'ordre du jour, dédié aux gastronomes parisiens, par un professeur, membre de plusieurs sociétés littéraires et savantes*. The author was Jean-Anthelme Brillat-Savarin, a bachelor and man of many parts, a gourmet who was independently wealthy. He survived the French Revolution, lived in the United States for a while, studied law, chemistry, and medicine, and was, moreover, as he advertised on his title page, a professor who belonged to several literary and learned societies. (Incidentally, he had a use for a truffle that involved not ice cream but roast beef.) His book, *The Physiology of Taste, or Meditations on Trancendental Gastronomy: A Theoretical, Historical, and Up-to-date Work, Dedicated to Parisian Gastronomes, by a Professor ... etc.,* was a series of stylized meditations, essays really, on the pleasures of the table, in which he included personal experiences, poems, and recipes.

In Meditation II, Brillat-Savarin tackled taste, breaking it down into sections of interest, analyzing the process of eating from the moment food passes under the nose to the second it reaches the tongue, and so on. He observed that there's very little taste without smell, and that smell is experienced at the back of the mouth. He offered simple experiments as proof. Pinching the nose between finger and thumb while eating was one. In doing so, he noted, "the sense of taste becomes curiously dulled and imperfect; by this means the most repulsive medicine may be taken almost without noticing." Pressing the tongue against the palate while swallowing was another technique: "the circulation of air is intercepted, the sense of smell is not aroused, and gustation does not take place." (As we all should begin in the dish and continue in your mouth to even greater effect, with saliva spreading the flavour all over your tongue. Brillat-Savarin preferred the image of a laboratory for the mouth, with the nose as its chimney. The laboratory breaks down the food. As for the chimney, well, that's where the *parfum* rises in a gastronomic cloud to your brain. A little fanciful, perhaps, but Brillat-Savarin was nothing if not the fanciful champion of a sophisticated palate.

It appears there are those fortunate few who are able to experience ice cream more vividly than the rest of us. John Harrison's great-grandfather owned two ice-cream parlours in New York City in the 1900s, his grandfather started the first dairy co-op in Tennessee, and his uncle owned an ice-cream factory in the South. So you could almost say he was born into his job. Every morning, Harrison arrives at Dreyer's Grand Ice Cream Co. in Oakland, California, dons a white lab coat, and begins to sample flavour after flavour. First, he allows the ice cream to melt a little, to warm up to 10 to 12°F, so his taste buds will receive a fuller message. Then he removes a small gold-plated spoon from his pocket and sets to work in earnest.

Beginning with the lighter flavours and moving on to the heavier, more intense and complex ones, he skims across the surface of an open container of ice cream with the spoon. Then he puts the spoon in his mouth and turns it upside down, allowing the ice cream to slide onto his tongue. He swirls it around, coating his taste buds, and, finally, smacks his mouth several times to warm the ice cream even more and beat some air into it.

The spoon is gold-plated because gold is inert and carries no taste of its own. Absolutely nothing must interfere with the taste of the ice cream. John Harrison doesn't drink coffee or alcohol. He doesn't smoke, and he avoids spicy foods. He takes care of his tongue since he's the official taster, the final quality check, and only when he gives his approval will the ice cream be shipped to consumers. This is his routine over a career of sampling from millions of gallons, and the way he describes it is enlightening. He claims he grew up on "the good taste of cream."

Only recently have scientists begun to consider the way taste and smell develop in childhood, even infancy. They know that babies who are breast-fed learn to prefer the flavours of their mother's diet. They've discovered that odour molecules vibrate within brain cells in the amygdala, the part of the brain that controls emotion. They're studying how intermingling makes it difficult to separate the signals of the senses of taste and smell. Anyway, the result is pure pleasure.

In an interview given to CBC Radio in 1991, Harrison said that he can detect the "top notes" in ice cream. "You taste in the middle," he observed, detailing the flavour associations of taste buds on specific regions of the tongue: on the tip, sweet; at the back, bitter; and on the sides, salty and sour. Now a new taste has been discovered, umami, a savoury taste associated with MSG. But, as Harrison explained, he's tasting the top notes with his nose. So the reason he rolls the ice cream around in his mouth is because he's looking for the bouquet, the aroma. And, just as wine tasters do with wine, he spits the ice cream out. "You don't need to swallow to taste it," he insisted.

The ice-cream company that employs him has taken out a $1-million insurance policy on John Harrison's tongue. It should have paid the same attention to his nose.

More facts:

According to W. S. Arbuckle, in *Ice Cream:* "The energy value and nutrients of ice cream depend on the food value of the products from which it is made."

According to Harold McGee, in *On Food and Cooking,* ice milk, sherbet, and fruit ices make up in sugar and

4

KINGS, COMMONERS, AND CONES

If you've ever made ice cream at home, you know how completely it becomes integrated into your life, how simple it is to have ice cream whenever you want it. There's the machine, for starters. These days, you don't need to go out and buy salt and ice for it. You know that something else you can't see does the trick in the walls of the insulated container. But there's no hint of the complex science involved, no explanation of the freezing agent in the handy booklet, complete with recipes, that comes along with it. The focus is on making ice cream, pure and simple.

One morning, a friend of mine dropped off his ice-cream machine so that I could try it. "Easy," he said. I stared at it. White base, white plastic dasher, a motor somewhere inside and an on/off switch—easy, indeed.

Through the clear plastic lid (resembling a cake lid) you could watch what was going on inside—fun too. It was then that I noticed how consciously designed the emphasis on fun really was. The hole in the lid was carved like a flower, resembling a daisy with nine petals. The top of the base looked as though a wave were circling it, perhaps to suggest the billows of ice cream that pushed up into view during the churning.

This was a user-friendly appliance. I was sure I could manage it and even use one of the recipes, one of the *basic* recipes, in the handy booklet. I whisked a cup of milk and 3/4 cup of sugar together, stirred in two cups of heavy cream and vanilla extract to taste—oh, I know, ice-cream connoisseurs use seeds and the vanilla pod—and poured the mixture through the hole in the lid into the chilled bowl that was waiting below. That was all there was to it. I turned on the machine and settled in to watch. Towards the end of twenty minutes, the ice cream did begin to inflate with air, fluff up and billow. Smooth white waves cresting above the bowl were all the proof I needed that my ice cream was forming.

Finally, into the freezer it went for ripening. Homemade slid in beside store-bought. If I could have peeked in the freezers along my street, I bet I would have found ice cream of both kinds in many of them. In the spirit of "a chicken in every pot," the campaign slogan of Herbert Hoover, today there's ice cream in every freezer—ready and waiting for the common man, woman, and child. The Western ideal.

I invoke a political slogan here because ice cream *has* been politicized throughout history, even been used as edible propaganda by warring sides. In World War I, the U.S. Army declared it a "morale food" for the troops, and the U.S. government called it an "essential foodstuff" for the folks back home. In World War II, it was considered too American by Japanese authorities, who discouraged its consumption and put sellers out of business by forcing a drop in the price of sundaes and sodas. In Italy, Mussolini banned the sale of ice cream outright. Apparently he too was afraid of American influence. When Italians fled fascism in the 1940s, they took their love of gelato with them all the way to Argentina, opening parlours there.

Clearly, ice cream has often been in the midst of the fray. And clearly it can be co-opted to deliver a message. Before the second Iraqi war, when Saddam Hussein was still in power, the *Detroit Free Press* reported, on June 12, 2002, that Iraqis were lining up to buy vanilla swirl ice-cream cones, topped with green, orange, and yellow syrup. There they were in Hurriya (Freedom) Square, under yet another enormous statue of the dictator. Though everything was in deadly short supply, Iraqis could still get ice cream. Or could they?

Months later, a different message was delivered. On December 20, 2002, *The Guardian* reported that the Baghdad Dairy had been forced to stop making ice cream because, under UN sanctions, it was not allowed to import a new centrifuge machine or certain chemicals and the machines and paper to make cartons. Even yeast had been banned. All these items were on the "goods review list" because they potentially had other uses—making missiles, making agents of chemical warfare. That's what can happen when ice cream is caught up in the cross-manipulations of power.

By the way, Hussein's favourite flavour is rumoured to be pistachio. The pistachio nut is the seed fruit of *Pistacia vera*, a tree that originated in the Middle East, in Persia. It grows in poor soil, with little rain, and its fruit is a delightful gift.

Well, give them their due. Princes and potentates—as well as dictators—have had their way with ice cream. They've given it their stamp, put it on the front lines, even taken it into battle. But though they've tried, they haven't been able to reserve it for themselves. In spite of armies and other trappings of power, they haven't been able to keep the dish, the cone, or the scoop exclusive. In this story, there's high life and low. All the while the high and mighty are ordering and eating, the humble are making ice cream—just as I did in my kitchen, just as the Iraqis carried on doing as long as they could, in spite of sanctions and Saddam Hussein—until, at last, in defiance of the game, with the kings in checkmate, there's ice cream for the pawns. A photograph in *The New York Times Magazine* of September 28, 2002, shows a young Afghani girl returning home from her local ice-cream parlour in Kabul. At the end of a bitter war, it's open again for business.

Let's say you enter an ice-cream gallery, hung with portraits of European rulers who've had a brush with ice cream. Their stories are known; their images are familiar. Their power and majesty have been immortalized in art. Yet in these lives a pattern is revealed: the slow, steady democratization of ice cream.

But I'm getting ahead of the tour. Just remember, as you set out, you're dealing with the centuries when ice cream was establishing itself in Europe. What was imagined or invented was intended to heighten interest and add glamour. That means you're in a gallery that mixes history and pseudo-history, according to well-established ice-cream tradition.

For example, in the gallery are paintings of two English monarchs, father and son, hanging next to each other on the wall. The father, Charles I, is said to have paid a lifetime pension to his confectioner provided the man kept his recipe for ice cream secret. The confectioner is even named. Actually, in various tellings of the story, he has several different names, none of which can be verified in the public record. You see, the story is make-believe. But there is a principle at stake, as his son, Charles II, duly recognized. With his father beheaded, and growing up in exile himself, he had every reason to be solicitous of power when he was restored to the throne. According to *The Institution, Law and Ceremonies of the Most Noble Order of the Garter* of 1672, at the Feast of St. George, in Windsor, on May 28 and 29, 1671, Charles II was served "one plate of white strawberries and one plate of Ice Cream." (If you're wondering about those "white strawberries," they were originally wild berries that were cultivated in the seventeenth century.) But notice that phrase: "one plate of Ice Cream." Here was an assertion of a divine gustatory right of kings. It was a right that soon became irrelevant, as the evidence shows.

Mrs. Mary Eales's Receipts, the first cookbook in English to contain a recipe for ice cream, appeared in 1718. Mrs. Eales had been confectioner to Queen Anne, and she recognized no restrictions on her freedom to divulge. Her recipe was basically cream, "either plain or sweeten'd," and a little fruit. Typical of her time, she didn't provide exact measurements. Mrs. Eales recommended placing pots of the ice-cream mixture into a pail, setting the pail atop straw and piling up ice and bay salt all around. Then, she said, "Lay a good deal of Ice on the Top, cover the Pail with Straw, set it in the Cellar where no Sun or Light comes, it will be froze in four Hours." There's no mention of churning. You know by now just how gravelly, how full of ice crystals, the result would be.

In a room by itself in the ice-cream gallery is a portrait of Catherine de' Medici, queen of France. In the invented portrait in this invented gallery, she holds not an orb or a sceptre but a goblet of *eau de violettes:* violet petals, water, and sugar, stirred and frozen a pale shade of mauve. In

1533, a fourteen-year-old Catherine left her native Italy to marry the duc d'Orléans. Three years after she arrived in France, when she was still a newcomer, an outsider, and a commoner, the dauphin François unexpectedly died. Catherine's husband inherited his brother's kingdom, and she became queen. However, the dauphin's death was attributed to poisoning by an Italian cup bearer, and Catherine's family was suspected in the plot. It didn't matter that the cup bearer confessed that he'd murdered the dauphin at the behest of someone else. Queen Catherine remained the Italian villainess in the eyes of the French. All this happened. But here's where legend takes over, and you arrive in ice-cream territory.

In the nineteenth century, long after old hatreds had been laid to rest, a tale circulated that Catherine brought her own confectioners with her when she arrived in France as a bride and that they had taught their French counterparts how to make ice cream—not simply for the court but for the public as well. In fact, Catherine lived and died before ice cream was available in France and before it was developed in Italy. So what's the point of the legend? For one thing, it represents a paradigm shift in the mythology of ice cream, in which Catherine has been transformed from villain into benefactor, and ice cream has left the palace for the haunts of the rising bourgeoisie. It's no accident that this legend was born in the nineteenth century, when the appeal of ice cream was spreading rapidly.

There remains one last portrait to see, that of Victoria Regina, queen of England, empress of India, in her full regalia of diamonds and black-tipped ermine. Victoria was an inadvertent benefactor—through her style more than anything else. At the Great Exhibition of 1851, dedicated to the latest in industry and technology, Queen Victoria attended a demonstration in the Crystal Palace conducted by Thomas Masters. He was a confectioner and author of *The Ice Book,* which he published in 1844, and he'd been working on developing a freezing machine for a long time. The one the queen saw was powered by steam, and it made artificial ice. It also made ice cream, one hundred quarts every fifteen minutes. Well, Victoria had a large family, and she presided over royal banquets. The way I imagine it, she might have turned to the Prince Consort and whispered to him behind her fan, "Dearest Albert, we must have this machine in our own home!"

The royal couple were devoted to domesticity, thereby creating a fashion for it, and homemade ice cream was just the thing for summer fêtes at Osborne House or entertainments at Windsor Castle, where Albert had made improvements to the dairy. Of course, Victoria didn't need to have Masters's machine to enjoy ice cream. There was the simpler ice-cream pail, an ice-cream maker produced by William Fuller at his Jermyn Street establishment. Fuller was already "ice pail maker to the Queen."

A menu from Windsor Castle shortly before her death in 1901 shows that Victoria was offered chocolate ice cream or lemon sorbet to round off her meal. She was inordinately fond of ice cream. Likely the treat was ordered from Messrs. Gunters', Confectioners to Her Majesty, Berkeley Square. But perhaps it was churned in the royal kitchens. In any event, Victoria could look back on her long life, satisfied that, by the example of her household, she had brought ice cream into the homes of the nation.

Into middle-class homes, that is. The goal was to achieve an ambience, even while eating ice cream, of which it could be said, "How like the family life of our own dear Queen." The lower classes weren't accommodated in this idealized setting of hearth and home, coziness and good cheer. But, at the very moment Victoria and her husband were watching the demonstration of Thomas Masters's machine in the Crystal Palace, peddlers were out on the streets of London selling a cheap, inferior ice cream to the masses. It might be made out of frozen turnip pulp rather than cream, but, if the masses could scrape up a penny or a ha'penny, they could buy it. Peddlers succeeded in creating an alternative reality with a very common touch. And they'd been doing it for some time, as early as 1820, not only in London but in Paris and New York City as well.

On second thought, maybe a portrait gallery is misleading in its portrayal of the concentration of power.

If I may adapt the words of the poet A. E. Housman, kings, queens, and itinerant street peddlers are "all equal made." No single one of them was responsible for the popularization and spread of ice cream. All of them were. The problem with the peddler is, he's difficult to track. He appeared not as an actor in the foreground but as part of the crowd. His name is usually lost because nobody cared to record it. Yet he was everywhere in the second half of the nineteenth century, when ice cream caught on quickly with all classes, when it really was a treat for the widest cross-section of people. And he began popping up in newspaper illustrations and in the transcription of his street cries. In Russia, as he trudged along, he advertised poppy-blossom ice cream and rose, along with the more usual flavours of chocolate, vanilla, and coffee. And he carried wooden tubs filled with ice, with metal containers of ice cream set in the centre, exactly as his fellows did in the United States.

Hokey-pokey, a penny a lump.
Hokey-pokey, find a cake;
hokey-pokey on the lake.
Here's the stuff to make you jump;
hokey-pokey, penny a lump.
Hokey-pokey, sweet and cold;
for a new penny, new or old.

That was the cry on American streets, and it became a rhyme for children who jumped rope as they chanted. There were variations on the rhyme—"The more you eat, the more you jump," or "The more you eat, the more you pump." As for the word *hokey-pokey*, it was a bastardized version of Italian and originated with street vendors who were probably shouting, "*Gelati! Ecce un poco!*" and "*Gelati! O che poco!*"—"Ice cream, here's a little! Ice cream, I have a little!" There was an Italian connection, all right.

Because of political upheaval in Italy in the nineteenth century, many vendors emigrated and became involved in their new lands with the ice-cream business. Those of Italian heritage engaged in it too. Selling ice cream was a way to make good. They toted buckets, pushed wheelbarrows, rang bells. Some of them had carts pulled by goats or bicycles, and they operated stands. The more successful among them owned cafés and restaurants. Carlo Gatti, an Italian-speaking Swiss, was one of the first to put ice cream on the menu, in a restaurant he opened in London in 1849. Two years later, he opened a stand near Charing Cross. As for the street vendors, their cry supplied the name by which they became known. They were the "hokey-pokeymen." And the word *hokey-pokey* became synonymous with ice cream. In the New World as well.

On a summer day, the amplified music from an ice-cream truck floats on the air. You recognize that it's coming from an ice-cream truck because it's a simple tune: "London Bridge Is Falling Down." The music box can also imitate old-fashioned chimes. Then the truck parks for a while, and the music stops. Right now, if you ran out to the street, you'd find customers beginning to gather, adults as well as children. Maybe there are orange blinking lights on top of the truck and a parade of dancing fudge bars, cones, and ice-cream sandwiches painted on the sides. The colours are bright, primary, the illustrations simple cartoons.

It strikes you that the vendor is really a descendant of those ice-cream peddlers of the past. His truck is decorated with the same goal of capturing attention. In 1820, for instance, a certain Lady Morgan came upon the stall of a vendor in Naples that she described as decorated with flowers and foliage, cupids and angels, with representations of the Madonna in heaven and sinners in purgatory, "and streaming with flags of gilt paper and red stuff." Lady Morgan also scrutinized the customers. "Half-naked beggars," she wrote (her disapproval patent), were trusted with a silver spoon. One by one, they ate their ices, and when they were finished, dutifully returned the spoon.

Of course, there wasn't always a spoon to be had. It was a luxury. In England, customers simply licked the ice cream, which came in what was called a penny lick, a cup with more glass than space inside, where quantity was an optical illusion. And, since the lick was rarely washed, it was implicated in outbreaks of tuberculosis and other diseases until it was finally outlawed, first in London in 1926, with other cities following suit. Much better to dish up the ice cream in something that wasn't shared.

The vendor leans over the counter in the side of his truck. "What'll you have?"

Take-away ice cream. That's what this street business is all about. You make your selection and hand your money over the counter.

"Okay," says the vendor, "here it is."

Enclosed in paper. Safe and sanitary on a stick.

In 1872, the Hokey-Pokey, a frozen fruit bar on a stick, was available, but it was ahead of its time. The idea didn't really catch on until about fifty years later, when Frank Epperson got the "novelty" going again—that's the term the trade still uses for pre-made, portable, individual treats. One night, Epperson, who manufactured powdered lemonade, left a full glass on the windowsill with a spoon in it. Overnight, the temperature dropped below freezing, and in the morning he realized that he'd produced something he could sell. He called it the Epsicle and patented it in 1924. The Epsicle became the Popsicle and proved an instant hit everywhere it was sold, in stands or stores or trucks, on city streets and boardwalks at the seashore, and in amusement parks. It was followed by the Creamsicle and all the other "sicles."

As for the Good Humor Bar, chocolate-covered ice cream on a stick, it was invented by Harry Burt of Youngstown, Ohio, in 1920. Burt was a confectioner who owned a candy store and was also something of an impresario. The name he chose for his novelty was meant to remind people of the link between body and soul—in Burt's terms, palate and mood. Eating one of his Good Humor Bars was supposed to improve your disposition and bring on a smile and a happy face. And Burt designed exactly the right street theatre to drive his message home. In the 1920s, at the wheel of a white truck, the Good Humor man began cruising neighbourhoods across America. He was instantly recognizable: dressed in a white suit, ringing a set of bells (borrowed from a bobsled), and dispensing frozen mood elevators.

"I grew up in Memphis, Tennessee," Gary Snow says. Snow is a neural psychologist, but right now he's talking about his love for ice cream. "I remember when the ice-cream man came around. I could hear the bells ringing. On a hot day, just the cooling sensation I'd get when the lid was opened—I could feel the cool, and I could see my ice cream coming towards me."

Good Humor men rang their bells. They were trained to deal with children. By the 1930s, they were also trained to deal with adults, raising their caps to ladies and saluting the men who'd come to buy. Their trucks and tricycles and pushcarts were spotless. They polished their shoes and took care of their nails. They were schooled in hygiene, traffic safety, and sales, a veritable army in white, the colour of milk. Obviously, ice cream had cleaned up its image from the bad old disease-ridden days. In the 1940s, in magazines, on radio shows, in comic strips and movies, the Good Humor men were celebrated as upright American heroes. All it took was a down payment of $100 for a franchise. The patent, however, ran out after World War II, and by the time the Good Humor trucks stopped rolling in the 1970s, they weren't the only ones on the road selling ice cream. Over time, all kinds of vehicles and companies had appeared, and they each offered their own selection of frozen delights.

"I remember there was a brief period, when I was a kid," Gary Snow says, "when some sort of motorized cart came around that looked like a small merry-go-round, with vivid lights and colours."

"What did you buy?" I ask him.

"Well, there were Popsicles and Creamsicles. There was also something called a Push Pop. I remember it as a tube that had sherbet in it. A little bit of the sherbet stuck up above the tube, and you would start eating that. When you got down to the cardboard surrounding the sherbet, you'd push it up and continue to the very bottom. Some Push Pops even had a toy at the bottom." He smiles at the memory.

The Push Pop that Gary Snow enjoyed so much is still around, still shaped like a tube, with cardboard underneath and encircling the sherbet (now it comes in at least two flavours). You still push up the cardboard bottom to raise the sherbet to the top.

But novelties come and go—it's in their nature—along with barrows, carts, even Good Humor trucks. And names change over time. For example, the hokey-pokeyman is known to most people today as the ice-cream man. Yet the experience he offers remains essentially the same. A picture from the *Illustrated London News* in 1872 shows a crowd of men, women, and children having a holiday on Hampstead Heath. They cluster, stand, and sit on the grass. In one corner of the picture, they swarm the seller who's behind his open cart, putting the ice cream expertly into the cups, shaping the swirls, making penny licks as

ICE-CREAM SELLER ON HAMPSTEAD HEATH

fast as he can. His sign advertises different sizes for different prices: one half-penny, one penny, two pence. If you think in terms of scoops, you're in the picture. Eating ice cream in public has become a shared, familiar hot-weather ritual.

One sultry late May evening some years ago, I remember joining a long line of customers outside an ice-cream parlour in Cambridge, Massachusetts. It was located in Harvard Square, opposite the university, so students in the queue, including myself, were talking about essays and exams while we waited our turn to buy an ice-cream cone, with or without jimmies (chocolate sprinkles on top). Or maybe we'd get a "frappe," Massachusetts slang for a milkshake. Though there were plenty of air-conditioned booths, few people were sitting inside. Those who'd already got what they came for seemed reluctant to leave. The connection between all of us was tenuous, light-hearted, circumscribed. No deep, searching questions or answers allowed. Merely a delightful hiatus in the usual custom of anonymity on the street.

When anthropologist Victor Turner wrote about pilgrimage, he used the term "liminality" (from the Latin *limen,* meaning "threshold") to describe the fluid, open existence of pilgrims. From the moment they left their front door until they reached their destination, they were part of a community that was constantly changing, always being re-formed. People on an ice-cream outing find themselves in that kind of liminal space. They join a band of strangers whom they're unlikely to meet again. Yet they interact with them, engage in conversation, and then continue on their way.

Behaviour can be uninhibited in this liminal space. The rules of etiquette about eating in public—not to open your mouth or produce a lot of noise when you're chewing, not to show your fangs—need not apply. I'm not suggesting that people turn into ravenous beasts. But, in this space where there's no danger, licence is granted. On that hot evening in Harvard Square, for example, cones were being masticated everywhere within earshot, and tongues and teeth were visible.

There is a catch. You have to realize you're in a liminal space for such freedom to exist. Otherwise, it's etiquette as usual. In the past, it seems, conduct was more regulated by convention. There's a piece of advice in Caroline Liddell and Robin Weir's book, *Frozen Desserts,* that illustrates the point. The gist is, a "gentlewoman" who's offered an ice-cream cone shouldn't eat it in public because she exposes her tongue when she licks it. That kind of behaviour, according to the anonymous adviser, marks her as a woman of "unsavory and unattractive appetites." Instead, she is to take the cone home, turn it upside down in a dish (the adviser, leaving nothing to chance, specifies a "shallow" dish), dispose of the cone and then tackle the ice cream with a spoon. Liddell and Weir don't provide the source or date of this wonderful piece of ice-cream memorabilia, but it dates itself to a degree. It has to have been penned around the turn of the twentieth century, when the ice-cream cone was new and people didn't know how to regard or manage it. Men were advised that it was effeminate to eat a cone; they had to learn to "manhandle" it. Still, there was safety to be found in society's codes and rules. Gradually the cone was assimilated into ice-cream life on the street, and the use and appreciation of it spread. But there remained pockets, especially rural communities, where it was unfamiliar.

Now a man in his seventies, with a career as a designer in mechanical engineering behind him, Steve (Stefan) Rausa had his first experience with an ice-cream cone at a fair in a small town in Slovakia in the 1930s. The way Steve remembers it, he was "only a toddler hanging on to his mother's skirt" as they strolled among the canvas-covered booths in the town square. When they arrived at an ice-cream stand, his mother suddenly stopped. "We'll have an ice-cream cone," she said.

I'd never had ice-cream cone before. The ice-cream man filled the cone and handed it to me. It was like sherbet, fruity, not creamy. My mother started walking again, and I continued eating. When I got down to the cone, I let go of her skirt. I didn't want to get too far from the ice-cream man because I thought I had to return the cone. [Shades of the penny lick.] So I used both hands to get all of the ice cream out of the cone. And then I took it back to the stand.

"You don't get any more," the ice-cream man told me. "You bite into that."

I didn't like the cone. It didn't taste like ice cream. When my mother found me, she was frantic: "Where have you been? What have you been doing?"

That brings me to the story of the arrival of the very first cone in the middle of a *world's* fair. The perfect setting for a liminal band of strangers who are ready to give it a try.

As its name implies, the Louisiana Purchase Exposition of 1904 celebrated the centennial of the vast territory the United States acquired from France. Held in St. Louis,

Missouri, the fair covered two square miles and comprised more than two hundred buildings for exhibits. John Philip Sousa conducted his band music there. The largest organ was built and installed in the grand Festival Hall. On view were an airplane, a radio, and a silent movie. There were also a butter sculpture of Teddy Roosevelt, a bear made out of prunes, and, in a small "reservation," Igorot tribesmen from the Philippines displayed as "savages." The fair was designed to celebrate progress, technology, and healthy living, but it also endorsed cultural imperialism. Anthropological exhibits extolled the superiority of civilized white men and the inferiority of everyone else. In other words, the fair was a heady mix of crude and cultivated, prejudiced and enlightened. And the exhibits spilled over onto Pike Street, "with its hurly-burly of foreign people," as a contemporary reviewer noted. "The Pike" was a midway with sideshows.

It so happens that among the "hurly-burly of foreign people" on the Pike was Abe Doumar, from Syria. As a teenager, he'd emigrated to the United States and worked at fairs around the country. When the World's Fair opened in 1904, he was in his twenties. Dressed in Arab clothing, Doumar sold souvenirs by day—paperweights were his most successful item, filled with water supposed to have come from the River Jordan. At night, he became a *zalabia* (a kind of crisp waffle) salesman, and he got an idea that could turn his penny waffle into ten cents' profit. He rolled the still warm *zalabia* into a cone and added ice cream to it. Abe Doumar called what would become the most American of treats "a kind of Syrian ice-cream sandwich" and shared his inspired idea with other vendors. The idea spread rapidly through the concessions. Well and good, except another *zalabia* salesman at the fair gave a different account of what had occurred.

In an interview published in *The Ice Cream Trade Journal* in May 1928, Ernest Hamwi said that his stand was located next to an ice-cream stand that ran out of clean cups. So Hamwi had come to the rescue with his *zalabia,* which was soon dubbed the "World's Fair cornucopia." Well and good again, except there were yet other claimants. The Kabbaz family, also from Syria, was sure that brothers Nick and Albert Kabbaz, who may have worked for Hamwi in his concession, were the real inventors of the cone. And Charles Robert Menches maintained that it was *he* who rolled the first two cones in *his* stand. (Incidentally, Menches and his brother Frank were the creators of Cracker Jack.)

If all these would-be inventors weren't enough, Turkish claimant David Avayou said he'd seen ice cream being eaten in France from paper and metal cones and simply substituted an edible one at the fair. Obviously, a close and intensely competitive little group. Take your pick of winner in the cone sweepstakes. Most everyone has.

In 1954, the International Association of Ice Cream Manufacturers gave its seal of approval to Ernest Hamwi, even though there's no record or photograph of Hamwi's *zalabia* stand at the St. Louis Fair. My favourite candidate remains Abe Doumar, who was such a showman. His family preserved a cone-making machine dating back to 1905, when it was used at Doumar's Coney Island ice-cream stand. Along with photographs and parts of that machine, Doumar's nephew Albert sent a mimeographed copy of "The Saga of the Ice-cream cone" (which he'd written) to the Smithsonian Institution. And in 1972 Albert appeared on the television program *To Tell the Truth,* making the case for his uncle as the cone's originator. Still, that really wasn't the beginning of the saga.

Priority was the name of the game. In 1903, Italo Marchiony of New York City filed for a patent to mould ice-cream cups, though they weren't edible. But he let it be known that in 1896 he'd begun selling cups made out of waffles and filled with his own lemon ice from a cart down on Wall Street. Then there was Antonio Valvona of Manchester, England, who in 1902 patented a device for making biscuit cups for ice cream. As early as 1820, however, in his cookbook, *The Italian Confectioner,* G. A. Jarrin described almond wafers that were rolled, covered with currants, and powdered with sugar. Obviously, they could also be used for holding ice cream. So could the rolled waffle-cornet oozing flavoured whipped cream that was devised by Charles Ranhofer. Chef at the celebrated New York restaurant Delmonico's, Ranhofer included his recipe in his cookbook, *The Epicurean,* in 1894. Also deserving consideration, surely, is the cornet filled with vanilla ice cream mixed with dried fruits, cinnamon, ginger, and Maraschino liqueur that Mrs. A. B. Marshall presented in her 1894 cookbook, *Fancy Ices.* Mrs. Marshall's cornet was piped with royal icing, dipped in chopped blanched pistachio nuts, and frozen, producing a dessert that must have been as rich and heavy as Victorian furniture. Never mind; the cone, the cornet, the cornucopia evolved to everyone's taste.

After the St. Louis Fair, entrepreneurs rushed in to invent cone-making machines, displacing the hand-rolled variety. The machines mixed the batter, squirted it into moulds, and packed the finished product off in boxes. By the late 1920s, millions of people were buying and eating some of the new and improved designs. Elaborate models were created—spiral cones, dripless cones (with a receptacle made out of candy), cones that held two scoops of ice cream side by side. But the basic cone, usually pointed, sometimes flat, made out of cake, waffle, and, eventually, sugar, triumphed over them all. It's the most recognizable. You can take it anywhere. And you can finish it in an average of about fifty licks. The ice cream in a single-scoop cone, that is. Yes, somebody out there has actually counted the licks.

As writer L. Rust Hills demonstrated in *The New Yorker* magazine of August 24, 1968, the etiquette for coming to terms with the cone has remained an issue. Hills gives a tongue-in-cheek explanation of how to get the cone under control and handle those pesky drips. Expertise lies in the rotation of the wrist, the strategic movement of thumb and forefinger, the pressure of the mouth and tongue on ice cream in a device with a mind of its own. Pleasure lies in bending it to your will.

Nobody but you can count the number of ice-cream cones you've consumed over the course of your life so far, or how many memories you associate with them. But, on a summer evening, chances are that all those other people walking along the street beside you, eating and managing their cones, have memories they bring along too. The cone has become the most popular icon of an ice cream culture.

A long time ago, at a garage sale, I picked up a plastic vanilla ice-cream cone. It's about two feet long and a foot wide at the scoop. It's hollow and has a flat rim, in which holes are placed strategically for nails to be driven through, and the cone is embossed with a cross-hatched design, just as real cones are, with the name of a well-known ice-cream company emblazoned on the front. The scoop is furrowed and swirled in waves of vanilla. The representation looks as though it might have been designed to hang outside a variety store in the 1950s, doing the job of a sign, unambiguously advertising what's for sale inside. I've kept the plastic cone to this day because of the memories it conjures up in my life. And I guess somebody kept it before me for much the same reason. When I show it to friends, it's as though we were standing outside a local variety store or by an ice-cream stand, and there we meet our earlier, unedited selves.

"My memories are of summers past," art critic Robert Enright says. "I was raised in Saskatoon. It has the most dizzyingly beautiful summers, high-skied, brilliant, everything etched in your imagination as well. I think of softball diamonds. I'd begin to salivate when I heard that bell ringing and the truck came by. There's nothing better than an ice-cream cone, baseball, and a hot summer day on the Canadian high prairie."

Recalling his small town in Slovakia and the day he ate his very first cone, Steve Rausa, the designer, tells me, "I remember that people got along with each other." He can still picture the town square, the church, the stream, and the grey stone bridge where the ice-cream stand was located. "It's the only place I use as a template. It seemed the life was full."

You realize what's taking shape in their words: a world as bright and innocent as the pictures on the side of an ice-cream truck. A world in which initiation is social as well as sensual and happens early. "Ice cream has the potency that certain songs do," Robert adds. Maybe that's what makes the image of the cone iconic. Then again, since memories are so very particular, it's also what makes the image personal.

"Memory's a process of construction and reconstruction," says Gary Snow, the neural psychologist. "Penfield stimulated various parts of the brain, eliciting memories of events. But what you elicit down the road over time is probably not the real, original experience." He is referring to Wilder Penfield, the Canadian neurosurgeon whose work revealed—at least to Penfield—that events left complete and permanent imprints on the brain. Except it turns out that memories are not really imprints of reality and certainly not complete. They're more like impressions, and what we hold on to is the meaning we give to them.

"I can still remember what I think to be the velvety taste to the chocolate ripple I had when I was a child in Tennessee," Gary says. "I insist, it was more flavourable when I was a child."

"I remember eating ice cream and pickles when I was thirteen," says Robert Enright. "I liked pickles."

"I remember the ice-cream man at the fair used a sort of wooden spatula to fill the cone. Not a scoop," Steve Rausa volunteers. "Also, there was a ride for children, like a carousel ride, but without a motor, and teenage boys pulled it around with one hand in a loop of rope. And there was music."

So the past may be captured in a sound or a taste or a visual detail or two. But it's always mediated, refracted, interpreted, shaded.

Early in his career, Andy Warhol did a sequence of ink-and-wash drawings of luscious food, lobster dinners, fruit baskets, extravagant picnic spreads. These were assembled into a little book called *Yum, Yum, Yum,* published after the artist's death. On the cover is one of his ice-cream cones, a flat and fanciful double dip. A pink scoop peeks shyly from behind a blue one, and the cone is ornamented like the basket of a balloon airship. It evokes very little response in the viewer, at least if that viewer is me.

"He was trying to flat-line meaning," explains Robert Enright, turning back into the art critic. "It doesn't work. I think Warhol found the ice-cream cone too loaded, too familiar an image because it's tied to the experience of everyone who's looking at the art."

Robert tells me that the sculptor Claes Oldenburg had once planned to erect a monumental chocolate-mint Good Humor Bar as an arch over New York's Fifth Avenue. The bar was meant to have a giant bite taken out of it for the traffic to pass through—Oldenburg's known for his humour. And it's evident in another of his ice-cream sculptures, this one installed in Cologne, Germany, in 2001. "Dropped Cone" is described as "built out of stainless and galvanized steels, fiber-reinforced plastic, balsawood" and "painted with polyester gelcoat." Practical, down-to-earth materials. The sculptor's wit consists in the conceit. The giant cone looks as if it has fallen from the sky, plummeting, the way cones do, straight down, bottoms up. As if some celestial hand let it go. But the cone has been stayed in its fall by the corner of a multi-storied building. A single scoop of ice cream is mashed against the edge. All 32 feet of the sculpture rise into the air above the building, far above the street below. Size has made Oldenburg's sculpture surprising and so has place-ment, and it may raise some playful theological questions. But the experience of dropping an ice-cream cone is promptly understood and shared by all who see his piece. The artist is dealing with memory, not fighting it, and it seems to me that's how it should be. The image isn't detached from its real-life roots.

In the twentieth century, in an attempt to capture American experience particularly, the cone has been turned into pop art. But I happen to have a more personal and

CERAMIC ICE-CREAM CONE

eccentric use of the image, a ceramic cone made by artist David Gilhooly in the 1970s. It's life size. You can hold it as you would a real cone, and it also looks like the real thing, with the colour, texture, and shape of its inspiration ... until you notice, sandwiched between two scoops of ice cream (one peppermint, the other maple walnut), a white, flecked with peppermint, and ribboned with green—frog. Grinning, hoppy, obviously glad to be there.

In 1945, a 3,500-cubic-foot helium balloon, touted as the largest in the world at 44 feet high and 16 feet wide, was made to resemble a triple-decker ice-cream cone. It was set bobbing, floating, and weaving above the crowd at the Macy's Thanksgiving Day Parade in New York City. The balloon was symbolic of the consuming passion for ice cream in the U.S.A. According to recent statistics, Americans, per capita, devour 23.8 quarts of ice cream a year, one ton in a lifetime, enough to fill the Grand Canyon. Canadians aren't far behind, consuming, per capita, a prodigious 18.8 quarts a year. But ice cream is pre-eminently an American love story, and it began early in the history of the Republic. There's a reference to ice cream in the description of a dinner for Maryland's governor in 1774.

Nobody knows for sure who introduced ice cream to the young United States—the French, Italians, or British. In his *Physiologie du goût (The Physiology of Taste)*, Jean-Anthelme Brillat-Savarin observed that when he was living in the United States in 1794–95, the women of New York City "never tired of a pleasure so novel to them; nothing was more amusing than to watch them smirk and simper as they tasted it. They could not understand how it could be kept so cold." Brillat-Savarin was more interested in recording the success of his compatriots in exile, Frenchmen who made their living by making and selling ice cream. But he couldn't resist the opportunity to mock the unsophisticated natives who were eating it.

Well, soon enough Americans became adepts as well as enthusiasts. And France and the French proved a natural resource. Thomas Jefferson developed his taste for ice cream while he was ambassador to France. In Paris, he employed a chef who made vanilla especially for him. Jefferson was very partial to vanilla, and we still have a detailed recipe for it in his own hand.

....

PRESIDENT JEFFERSON'S VANILLA ICE CREAM

2 bottles of good cream

6 yolks of eggs

1/2 lb. sugar

Mix the yolks & sugar.

Put the cream on a fire in a casserole, first putting in a stick of Vanilla. When near boiling take it off & pour it gently into the mixture of eggs & sugar.

Stir it well.

Put it on the fire again, stirring it thoroughly with a spoon to prevent its sticking to the casserole.

When near boiling take it off and strain it thro' a towel.

Put it in the Sabotière [sorbetière].

Then set it in ice an hour before it is to be served. Put into the ice a handful of salt. Put ice all around the Sabotière, i.e. a layer of ice a layer of salt for three layers.

Put salt on the coverlid of the Sabotière & cover the whole with ice.

Leave it still half a quarter of an hour.

Then turn the Sabotière in the ice 10 minutes.

Open it to loosen with a spatula the ice from the inner sides of the Sabotière.

Shut it and replace in ice.

Open it from time to time to detach the ice from the sides.

When well taken (prise), stir well with the spatula.

Put it in mould, jostling it well down on the knee.

Then put the mould into the same bucket of ice.

Leave it there to the moment of serving it.

To withdraw it, immerse the mould in warm water, turning it well till it will come out & turn it into a plate.

Ice cream was often on the menu at the White House. George Washington was wild about it and had it served frequently at his dinners and levées. Dolley Madison gave ice cream cachet by featuring it at a dinner celebrating the second inauguration of her husband, James, in 1813. Presidents Andrew Jackson, Herbert Hoover, Richard Nixon were devotees. Franklin Delano Roosevelt declared he had to have ice cream at least once a day, and chocolate was his favourite. No doubt Roosevelt offered maple and almond to George VI when he came to dine because they were the king's favourite flavours. So much for presidents and kings.

In the best American tradition, the power lies with the people. Where do you think Dolley Madison got her recipe for ice cream? According to legend, from Aunt Sallie Shadd, a former slave from Wilmington, Delaware, who was famous among the free-black population there as the inventor of ice cream. The First Lady is supposed to have headed straight for Wilmington to get the recipe from the source. Well, that may be fiction, but this much is fact. In the late 1820s, an African-American named Augustus Jackson left his position as cook at the White House and moved to Philadelphia, where he started his own catering business and distributed his own ice cream to local street vendors, many of whom were also African-American. By the time the century was over, prejudice forced them out of the ice-cream business, but, for a while, equal opportunity prevailed.

Here are some snapshots from more than a hundred years of American ice cream history. In New York City in 1828, the press reported that street vendors were using a brand-new cry, "I Scream Ice Cream." In 1927, that cry would be incorporated into the chorus of a popular song, "I Scream, You Scream, We all Scream …" Well, you know the rest. The Temptation I-Scream Bar, invented by Christian Nelson, cashed in on the song before its name was changed to Eskimo Pie. In the 1930s, *Kid Millions,* a movie starring Eddie Cantor, ended in an ice-cream factory, with chorus girls dancing on a giant freezer. In the 1940s, Victory sundaes were patriotic. In the 1950s, supermarkets were stocking ice cream bricks. Then came the 1960s. To celebrate the successful flight of *Apollo 13,* flavours called Lunar Cheesecake and Moon Shot were launched. Andy Warhol went on television to advertise a sundae named after him in colours of puce, magenta, chartreuse, and mauve. I could continue, but you get the point. Through all the decades, ice cream has been integral to the American way of life. It's had its ups and downs but has never disappeared.

It has even had the role of goodwill ambassador. In 1921, the commissioner of Ellis Island offered ice cream to immigrants as part of their first meal in the United States. The newcomers thought it was butter and began spreading it on their bread with knives. Today, American ice cream travels the world. Large quantities of it are exported to Japan, which began Westernizing in the nineteenth century and rapidly Americanized after 1945. In this regard, I offer you a small vignette.

One evening in Toronto, at a restaurant called Mikado, I'm enjoying a Japanese meal of sushi. The proprietor, Keiichi Masuda, smokes his own eel. He is an artist among artists in this particularly traditional food from his country. However, I want to talk to him about ice cream, specifically the Japanese attitude towards it after World War II. After all, ice cream had been so closely associated with the enemy, and not just in that conflict. Ever since 1851, when Jacob Fussell began supplying Union troops during the Civil War, ice cream has been an essential part of the American military diet. During World War II, for example, the U.S. Navy outfitted one of its barges as an ice-cream parlour, producing 10 gallons every second for the sailors. So after the war, when the American occupation of Japan began, ice cream inevitably re-entered the country with the occupiers.

Keiichi Masuda is a child of post-war Japan. I ask him if he remembers his earliest experience with ice cream. He smiles at me from under the headband of a sushi chef, hesitates, apologizes for his English. "When I was a kid," he says, "ice cream very expensive. But when I was fifteen, I went many times to American navy base and had soft ice cream."

There's nothing *more* American. J. F. "Grandpa" McCullough and his son, H. A. "Alex" McCullough, from Green River, Illinois, preferred the taste of ice cream immediately after it was made, before its final freezing— semi-solid, or soft, in other words. The McCulloughs began producing and selling their soft ice cream in 1938 under the logo "Dairy Queen." But it wasn't until after the war that it became a craze in the United States. Everything on the navy base in Japan was up-to-date when young Keiichi Masuda was becoming acquainted with ice cream American-style.

The Americanization of the culture went only so far, however. Japan has always had its own way of combining foreign with familiar. Green tea ice cream is a popular dessert in Japanese restaurants both in Japan and North America, and it incorporates *maccha,* the green tea powder used in traditional tea ceremonies. The tea-green hue is paled by the white of what is at heart American vanilla ice cream. As a shortcut, you can just trickle green tea syrup over vanilla ice cream. Presto! Fusion.

In his book *Near a Thousand Tables,* historian Felipe Fernandez Armesto talks about global "foodstuff migrations," how chili, for instance, travelled from Mexico to Texas and became "Tex-Mex." He's talking about trade in spices, sugar, tea, and coffee—but ice cream has travelled its own trade routes. Take the case of pistachio ice cream, which is a marriage of ground pistachios and vanilla ice cream. The nut was introduced into the United States at the end of the nineteenth century by Syrian immigrants, and the melded flavour was the inspiration of an American in 1940.

Tyrants take note. Everything's transient, including power. "There is no emperor but the emperor of ice cream" goes the line from the poet Wallace Stevens. Ice cream has crossed borders, been banned and reintroduced, been influenced by local traditions and reinvented. In the end, nothing can prevent ice cream from reaching the people.

5

SHOW BUSINESS

In her book about Paris in the 1890s, *Elegant Wits and Grand Horizontals,* the American writer Cornelia Otis Skinner included a remarkable vignette. It concerned a wealthy baron by the name of Monsieur de Saint-Crick. Every afternoon, he used to visit the famous restaurant Tortoni's. He'd sit at a table outside the restaurant and order two different kinds of ice cream—strawberry and vanilla. And when they arrived, he'd remove his shoes and put the vanilla into the right one and the strawberry into the left. If he got the arrangement wrong, he'd start all over again, first taking care to empty his shoes on the pavement.

When it comes to ice cream, show business is about showing off. But it's also about attention to detail, as you can tell from the example of Monsieur de Saint-Crick. The flavours had to be the same each afternoon, and one shoe wouldn't pass for the other. Right is right, and left is left. The baron devised a kind of choreography for the event that took place in full view of his fellow Parisians. Perhaps, nowadays, what he was doing would be labelled performance art. At any rate, he was an intrepid artist of eccentricity, and he certainly was all on his own. Nobody'd want to share.

The baron chose the right setting for his ice-cream exhibitionism. Tortoni's was founded in 1804 by a Neapolitan ice-cream maker who gave it his name. He invented *biscuit Tortoni:* frozen cream mousse (the cream is whipped) with macaroons, almonds, and rum. But clearly the artistry didn't end with Tortoni or his café. Ice cream has been a medium of expression for some of the best chefs in history, as well as for amateurs whose inspiration carried their dish to stardom. Such artistry has always required a heightening of effect and glamour in the presentation. So this chapter begins with what could be called signature pieces, treated not in chronological order but in terms of the show they put on. This isn't your everyday ice cream. It's been all dressed up to meet the public.

Great chefs can make ice cream represent more than itself. They can fabricate a work of the imagination akin to a poem, a song, or a sculpture because, as Aristotle observed in the *Poetics,* "The greatest thing in style is to have a command of metaphor." The goal is to make art that will be remembered. And because of biographies and autobiographies, how the chefs have done it, and *that* they've done it, is memorialized. Georges Auguste Escoffier was dubbed "the emperor of chefs" by Wilhelm II, the emperor of Germany. When he was a child growing up in Provence, Escoffier loved to draw; in fact, he wanted to be an artist. But his father decided that a trade would be more practical, so Escoffier went into cooking and applied his talent there, developing a taste for simplicity that would be his signature.

In 1891, Escoffier was chef at the Savoy Hotel in London. He was working on a surprise, an ice-cream confection, for the celebrated Australian soprano Nellie Melba. Inspired by her role as Elsa in Wagner's opera *Lohengrin,* he'd fashioned a swan out of ice to represent Elsa's brother, who, in the opera, is turned into a swan. Escoffier placed the ice swan on a silver platter and covered it with delicate spun sugar. Between its wings, he set both peaches that had been poached in vanilla syrup and vanilla ice cream. Escoffier entitled his creation *les Pêches au Cygne*. He was nothing if not theatrical. You can almost hear Wagner's music playing in the background, accompanied, no doubt, by murmurs of appreciation from the assembled dinner guests when the dessert was grandly presented to the diva. The swan's graceful, elongated neck curved, its head inclined as though it were alive, its body appeared to float on a silver lake.

Eight years later, on July 1, 1899, to celebrate the opening of the Carlton Hotel in London's Haymarket, Escoffier added raspberry purée to the dish and had it served up to Melba again. This time she inquired about its name, and Escoffier had another thought. He asked her if he could call it *Pêche Melba*. Canny chef! Perhaps he knew the singer worried that eating ice cream too often might damage her vocal chords. At any rate, disarmed by his flattery, she assented to the name. So it went down in history, everyone agreeing that the addition of the purée gave the dessert its distinction.

Pêche Melba is still on menus today—oh, so simple and delicious, a combination of peaches, tenderly poached, raspberry purée, and vanilla ice cream. But what's missing now is the original show business: the ice swan, the silver lake, the *mise en scène*. It's too labour intensive for our pared-down times, I guess, or possibly too Victorian. Nevertheless, from Escoffier's point of view, it was crucial. Replete with allusions to opera, to Melba's career, even to the grace and beauty of nature, the swan was more than a swan. It was the chef's master stroke.

According to the philosopher Edmund Burke, there are the senses, and then there's the imagination, "to which belong wit, fancy, invention and the like; this faculty, though it cannot produce anything absolutely new, varies the disposition of the ideas received from the senses … It is addicted to resemblances, and thus develops similitudes, metaphors and analogies, which appeal immediately to all men." That's from Burke's *A Philosophical Inquiry into the Origin of Our Ideas of the Sublime and the Beautiful.* It seems, when Escoffier carved his swan, he was participating in a grand enterprise: that of making "similitudes, metaphors and analogies" out of ice.

This kind of sculpture dated back at least to the seventeenth century in Europe and was popular in palaces from Rome to Versailles. And wherever the imagination went, it created centrepieces that were mountains, columns, obelisks, pyramids, precedents for monumental ice-cream sculpture to come. At a dinner in Rome in 1623, for example—as described by Antonio Frugoli in his *Pratica e Scalcaria* (Art and Practice of Stewardship)—guests were treated to a *monte di diaccio con diversi frutti dentro,* a "mountain of ice with diverse fruits within." While the fruit gleamed from the icy depths, orange flower water spouted out the top, perfuming and cooling the air around. Nothing was freehand, you understand. These elaborate ice sculptures were formed with moulds, sometimes with inner and outer chambers, designed by intricate engineering.

The next step was obvious. Why not fill the moulds with ice cream? Of course it was far more complicated to work with than ice, involving many ingredients and stages. Everything had to come together at just the right moment, lest a structure melt and collapse too soon. Nevertheless, the skills needed to manage the outcome were soon learned. And, with the help of the moulds, ice cream began passing itself of as all manner of things, from architecture to counterfeit food. A most ingenious deception was practised in the latter part of the eighteenth century by the nuns of San Gregorio Armeno, a convent in Naples. The nuns skilfully moulded, unmoulded, and

ICE CREAM

ICE-CREAM MOULDS
1 TRAFALGAR BOMBE
2 PINEAPPLE BOMBE
3 TOGO BOMBE
4 CONGO BOMBE
5 SNOWMAN
6 BOMBE CECILIE
7 BASKET OF ORANGES
8 WINDMILL
9 CHESS BOARD
10 TURBAN
11 BOMBE ISABELLA
12 BOMBE MARIE-LOUISE
13 CROWN
14 BOMBE MAGNOLESKOV
15 OTHELLO BOMBE
16 CHAMPAGNE COOLER

coloured a groaning board of fakes: hams, fowl, and fish made out of ice cream. The cold collation was designed for the pleasure of the Sicilian king and queen and their entourage. When the queen cut into a slice of cold turkey, she was surprised to discover that it was a slice of lemon ice instead.

Ice cream could fool, deceive, and enchant by resembling what it was not. It could give rise to a fantasy. And, since it was edible, the fantasy could be consumed in the most agreeable of ways. What a fascinating comment on the act of creation, on the power to make and unmake what the imagination conceives. It was an aesthetic arising out of the nature of ice cream itself. Because it is always at risk of melting before it even reaches the mouth, its own annihilation is inherent. Destruction is part of the spectacle.

You can still find antique moulds that recall the frozen masterpieces of the past. The moulds were usually hinged and heavy, to retain the cold longer and to allow for a successful, speedy release of the ice cream. They were shaped to make the ice cream look like fruit *(fruits glacés),* or cheese *(fromages glacés),* or vegetables, a boar's head, or a tongue. Some resembled stars, crenellated towers, minarets, spires. Since they were usually made of lead-based pewter, most of the old moulds are unsuitable for use today. They're collector's items, moulds of birds, people, snowmen, animals, even teddy bears.

By the twentieth century, French, English, German, Austrian, and American manufacturers advertised moulds that were associated with the celebration of holidays. But the nineteenth century remains the heyday. It seems there was no limit to what ambitious chefs and confectioners could do with their moulds, playing with form, painting on colour for realism and gold leaf for opulence, decorating their final compositions with leaves, vines, hats, flags. In Marcel Proust's novel *In Search of Lost Time,* Albertine is passionate about ice cream that's contoured as an edifice or a landscape: "Whenever I eat them, temples, churches, obelisks, rocks, a sort of picturesque geography is what I see before converting its raspberry or vanilla monuments into coolness in my gullet." There it is again, the theme of destruction, right down the eater's "gullet."

Albertine mentions that the ambitious shapes she prefers were already out of style in her world; much as she adores them, she describes them as "old-fashioned." Yet simpler moulds persisted and were known (as they still are) as bombes. The word found its way into English from the French; the Italian word *bomba* has the same application. It refers to the shape of the mould—

spherical, cylindrical, like a bomb. The contents are its payload, then, exposed when a bombe is opened up with a knife. In the nineteenth century, you could fill a mould shaped like an artillery shell or an anarchist's projectile, complete with flames of spun sugar—very popular in the latter part of the century. Ice cream was taking the mickey out of war.

There are many contemporary recipes for bombes. But be forewarned: they're difficult to make, even if you're using plastic bowls in place of the old difficult hinged moulds. They require layering of different kinds of ice cream, sorbets, and mousses, and freezing them progressively. Air pockets must be avoided. So unless you're feeling up to a challenge, perhaps they're best left to the experts.

You can always order an ice-cream cake that looks like Cinderella or a railway train for your child's birthday—in place of the customary scoop of ice cream at the side of the cake. Or you can have a wedding catered with little moulded ice-cream fruits. St. Clair Ice Cream in Toronto sells these special treats, and St. Clair Ice Cream in South Norwalk, Connecticut, will ship them. With reverence for the splendour of the past, St. Clair uses aluminum reproductions of antique pewter moulds. Strawberries, walnuts, day lilies, seashells, Yule logs, corn on the cob, golf balls, Easter eggs, your wish is their command.

Every showman knows there has to be a hook. And there was never a better showman than Charles Ranhofer. From 1862 until 1876, he was chef at Delmonico's restaurant in Union Square in New York City. Ranhofer was a Frenchman, an autocrat and ambitious in the kitchen, and when it came to ice cream, he was a master, using moulds to fashion tomatoes that weren't tomatoes, potatoes that weren't potatoes, bananas that weren't bananas. Just for fun and to flex his creative muscles, he might offer a frozen showpiece that was a little scene—for instance, a hen with chicks or eggs in her nest, made out of burnt almond ice cream, chocolate icing, spun sugar, and sponge cake. When the United States acquired the territory of Alaska from Russia in 1867, Ranhofer found himself wondering whether he could capitalize on the event and produce something novel, exciting, and celebratory all in one. "Alaska is cold, very cold, in winter," perhaps he thought. So how could he make ice cream—an appropriate medium, all things considered—defy or appear to defy its natural tendency to melt?

And then he had it: a confection that resembled an inverted cone. He would mould a Savoy biscuit as the base, hollowing out the centre and lining it with apricot marmalade. Inside the biscuit, he would add a layer of banana ice cream followed by a layer of vanilla ice cream, then keep the confection frozen until the last possible minute. Finally, he would cover the cone with meringue and brown it rapidly in a hot oven. That's basically Ranhofer's recipe for a dessert that appeared in his 1894 cookbook, *The Epicurean,* and is now known as baked Alaska. He actually dubbed it "Alaska, Florida," maybe because of the short, intense heating process involved, or maybe because of the cake and marmalade that embraced the ice cream without causing a meltdown. The chef was exploiting contrast.

But it seems somebody had been exploring that territory before him. A number of people, actually. On February 6, 1802, Thomas Jefferson treated his guests in the White House to ice cream in hot pastry. As one contemporary account put it, "Very good, crust wholly dried, crumbled into thin flakes; a dish somewhat like a pudding." If you enjoy mysteries, however, there is a very intriguing earlier sighting of something like a baked Alaska. It involves a man with a complicated résumé.

Benjamin Thompson was born in Massachusetts in 1753. He became a spy for the British during the American Revolution, was briefly a statesman, and, in 1803, went to Paris, where he gave up spying and politics for good. Rewarded by the British with a title, Thompson, now Count Rumford, devoted his energies to scientific enquiry, including the study of heat. It seems he was a physicist who also liked cooking. He invented a dessert he called Omelette Surprise—basically, ice cream set in the middle of a meringue—and cited his own research proving that beaten egg whites were resistant to heat. Meringue was also Ranhofer's choice for a coating. Could he have been aware of Thompson's pioneering work in the kitchen and laboratory?

Then there was the column in the journal *Liberté* on June 6, 1866, written by the food writer Baron Léon Brise, who insisted that the concept was originally French by way of the Chinese. The baron explained that master cooks at the Chinese Mission in Paris taught French chefs at the Grand Hotel their recipe: vanilla or ginger ice cream with a pastry covering, baked in the oven. "The gourmets," he wrote, "can thus give themselves the double pleasure of biting through piping hot crust and cooling the palate on contact with fragrant ices." Just as Thomas Jefferson's guests had. Perhaps the baron was indulging in a little show business, imparting to the dish an exotic background. What this toing and froing about the globe reveals, however, is that the idea was most certainly in the air.

And it continued to inspire. In the 1880s, Jean Giroix, chef at the Hôtel de Paris in Monte Carlo, was locked in fierce competition with our old friend Auguste Escoffier, who was also working in Monte Carlo at the time. (Chefs are like orchestra conductors; they move around the world.) In the hopes of outdoing Escoffier, Giroix took a cake and cut it into the shape of an omelette. He slathered it first with a fruit or cream ice, then with a layer of meringue, and finally popped it into a very hot oven. In 1895, he introduced his *omelette norvégienne,* or Norwegian omelette, to lucky hotel patrons. "Norway is cold, very cold, in the winter," he must have thought.

Now two names existed for a similar dessert: one French—*omelette norvégienne* (Giroix's)—and the other American—Alaska, Florida (Ranhofer's). Both nations claimed to have invented the dish, reflecting a rivalry that extended beyond the kitchen and into other aspects of their respective cultures. The rivalry persists. In an article that looks at French anti-Americanism and also American "anti-Gallicism" (his term), writer Bill Grantham begins with a witty retelling of this history and adds a personal anecdote. When he was dining on a riverboat in Paris in 1986, an American at Grantham's table became angry. She complained that the menu, by featuring an *omelette norvégienne,* was being anti-American.

All's well that ends well. Baked Alaska was the name immortalized in Fannie Farmer's 1896 *Boston Cooking-School Cookbook,* replacing Ranhofer's slightly clumsy epithet. A good concept deserves to be imitated and adapted. At the 1893 Chicago World's Fair, fried ice cream was sold as Alaska Pie or Alaska Fritters. Fried ice cream is French. These days, it has also been showing up in Mexican restaurants, balls in a batter of egg and cornflakes, submitted to very hot oil for just one minute. There's Japanese ice cream tempura too.

Caramel, chestnut, chocolate, asparagus, cinnamon, ginger, cherry, currant, lemon, strawberry, raspberry, pistachio, peach, pumpernickel rye bread, tutti-frutti, apricot, nectarine, burnt almond, pineapple, rice, angelica, truffle, and white coffee—how many flavours is that? Twenty-three. Charles Ranhofer used all of them in his ice-cream recipes—but then, he was famous for variety. The fact is, ice cream seems able to accept and accommodate whatever is added to it, welcoming the earthy, savoury, and spicy as well as the sweet. It can be made to taste like fruit and vegetables. It can incorporate bread, as Ranhofer clearly knew, though he wasn't the first to seize on the possibility. A recipe for rye bread cream ice circulated in Paris a hundred years before Ranhofer even put on his apron. The great chefs of the nineteenth century inherited the idea of a palette of flavours, as varied as the colours in a painting.

Back in the middle of the eighteenth century, in Paris, the range of flavours was ambitious: strawberry, raspberry, red currant, rosehip, lemon, vanilla, pistachio, caramel, orange, peach, apricot, greengage, grape. There were almond, cherry kernel, tea and coffee cream ices, and rose and carnation sorbets, cited for medicinal properties. And, in the 1760s or thereabouts, ices flavoured with liqueur appeared.

Naturally, things were happening beyond the French capital. An eighteenth-century recipe for brown bread ice cream was popular in England—1/2 pint of brown bread-crumbs, 1 1/2 pints of cream, and sugar. But if you're getting the impression that Paris was a hub of ice-cream activity, you're right. For one thing, in the eighteenth century the proliferation of *café-glaciers*, or ice-cream parlours, brought about experimentation and imitation. Distillers, confectioners, and *limonadiers* (makers of lemonade) vied with each other to create the latest sensation, which the public then eagerly consumed. Flavours demonstrate prowess. In 1791, the *Encyclopédie méthodique des arts et métiers* listed eighty different flavours and flavour combinations.

Ice cream had come of age, and the idea and style of the *café-glacier* was *prêt-à-porter*. Italians, who had founded and ran some of the most famous cafés in Paris, opened them elsewhere in the world. And no matter where they went, they continued to devise recipes and adjust their ice creams to the tastes of their customers. If they sold gelati, for example (from the Italian *gelare,* "to freeze," and made with more eggs and milk and less cream than French ice cream), their establishment was known as a gelateria, a word that's ubiquitous today. But, more to the point, gelati—soft, dense, and intense in a myriad of flavours—are their legacy. There's no business like the show business of flavours, with its delectable harmonies, unexpected combinations, even clashes.

This is how the game begins: with four friends studying the menu in a gelateria. On the right side of the menu are the familiar Italian flavours: bacio, amaretto, tartufo. But on the left are more formidable selections, provocatively described.

"There's something called *Nervoso*—'nervous,'" says Gilbert. "Coffee ice cream sprinkled with chocolate chunks and smothered in chocolate sauce."

"The *Nervoso* comes on top of waffles or crêpes," May notices. "You can't just have it by itself."

We consider the sugar rush that would invade our bodies if we ate "nervous" ice cream. And then, as Sherlock Holmes would announce to Dr. Watson, "the game's afoot." Of course flavours come with associations, but we start making freer ones.

"I think Sigmund Freud would have preferred coffee ice cream," I say, thinking of Freud's love of coffee, strong, black, and steaming in a cup. In all honesty, I know of no reference in the works of Sigmund Freud to ice cream.

But I do recall his writing "Civilized Sexual Morality and Modern Nervous Illness."

Gilbert nods. "Neurotic ice cream."

"Would Freud like a cone or a cup?" asks Greg. "A cone would taste good as long as it was his father's."

"That's an Oedipal cone," Gilbert jokes.

Finally, we agree on what we think would be a more appropriate selection for Sigmund Freud, well suited to his life and work, edgy. It's a cup of black coffee with a scoop of vanilla ice cream in it and *Schlag,* whipped cream, on top. As far as the Austrians are concerned, they always have time for *Schlagobers.* Freud could get it at his regular coffee house in Vienna, the Café Landtmann, where ice cream is on the menu. Once, on a trip to Vienna, I stopped in and ordered two scoops of vanilla, with whipped cream, hold the coffee. The buzz lasted the entire day.

"Since we're in an Italian ice-cream parlour, what do you suppose Federico Fellini would have liked?" May asks.

Gilbert has spent time in Italy. "I think it's the *Dolce Sogno*—the 'luxurious dream.' It's a close as you can get to *La Dolce Vita*. Chocolate ice cream covered with marshmallows and nuts, smothered with chocolate and caramel sauce, topped with whipped cream."

By the time the waitress arrives to take our order, we've played the ice-cream association game with celebrated film directors, artists, writers.

"What would Jane Austen order?"

"Lemon ice."

Tennessee Williams? "Bitter chocolate, laced with bourbon." Salvador Dali? "Something with nuts."

I ask the waitress, "How many flavours do you have in all?"

"Eighteen," she tells me.

That's a modest number when competition is fierce. In this day and age, a machine called a variegating pump can inject ribbons, swirls, ripples, and revels into the mix. A fruit feeder can insert fruits, nuts, candy, and cookie bits, collectively known as particulates. And ice-cream makers, who now include food scientists in their ranks, set out to contrive flavours of every hue and description, velvety, grainy, or chunky, simply because they can.

The time-honoured basics of vanilla, chocolate, and strawberry coexist with flamboyant and outlandish arrivistes. Squash, mustard, sauerkraut, horseradish, and root beer have been developed by the Department of Dairy Technology at Ohio State University. In July 2002, the *Mainichi News* reported that, at an ice-cream exhibition in Tokyo, Japanese ice-cream makers tried to outdo the West by presenting their own "wacky" flavours, among them octopus, squid, shrimp, crab, eel, ox tongue, and cactus. In 2004, Japanese grocery stores were selling ice cream with the flavours of garlic, potato and lettuce, seaweed, and raw horse flesh.

There have been wizards in the field, among them Vince Misceo, owner of La Casa Gelato, an ice-cream parlour in Vancouver, British Columbia. He isn't a chemist. He's a guy who mixes a little of this with a little of that and tries to come out with something better; at least that's how he portrays himself. Misceo may be reticent about his talent, but he is indisputably a master. He uses only the finest ingredients in his ice creams, sorbets, and frozen yogurts, and, every year, he adds brand-new flavours to his list. Unusual and exotic flavours. In 1995, twenty-eight. In 1997, twenty. In 1998, thirty. And so it goes. Chili, wasabi, radicchio, basil Pernod, carrot, avocado, taro root, pear and Gorgonzola, red currant and jalapeño, longan and purple yam, lemon tarragon, ginger-garlic, chicken curry—people came from everywhere to discover how the chicken curry ice cream tasted. To date, La Casa Gelato has experimented with more than five hundred flavours, about two hundred of them in demand, and the number is climbing. Still, according to the Guinness Book of World Records, the Heladeria Coromoto, an ice-cream parlour in Merida, Venezuela, holds the record. It sells more than seven hundred flavours as of this writing. The favourite is sweet corn.

Dr. Alan R. Hirsch, director of the Smell and Taste Treatment and Research Foundation, in Chicago, conducted a study on flavours and personality types. Vanilla lovers, he found, tend to be the impulsive risk takers among us; they also happen to enjoy close family ties and have a busy schedule. Strawberry people are shy, skeptical, detail-oriented, opinionated, self-critical. Butter pecan lovers, ethical, competitive, fiscally conservative (does that mean they're cheap?). Chocolate aficionados are characterized as charming, ambitious, accomplished, creative. Who wouldn't want to be classed in that category? And yet, according to the International Ice Cream Association, vanilla ranks the highest in consumption, accounting for more than half of all ice cream eaten. And that, according to the Dairy Science and Technology Department of the University of Guelph, is because it's the basis of so many frozen treats: milkshakes, sundaes, banana splits. In addition, it graces pies, birthday cakes, and other desserts, à la mode.

The sources of flavours are as fascinating as their treatment. Vanilla comes from a plant related to the orchid family, *Vanilla planifolia,* indigenous to the New World. Each flower must be fertilized by hummingbirds or bees before it yields a bean that's picked, put into hot water, fermented for several months, wrapped in straw to sweat, then sun-dried. Next, the vanilla bean is aged for one to two years, deepening its colour and aroma. At the end of this long, labour-intensive process, the precious flavour, vanillin, is extracted. There *is* synthetic vanilla, a by-product of the pulp and paper industry, but I'll speak no more of that. The real stuff was first used by the Aztecs, as documented by the Spaniards in the sixteenth century. Montezuma was fond of *tlilxochitl,* a drink made from cacao beans and flavoured with vanilla. And you know what the cacao bean delivers. Chocolate.

The cacao bean is the fruit of the tree *Theobroma cacao,* an evergreen that grows in Mexico, Central America, South America, and the West Indies and on the west coast of Africa. (Our spelling, *cocoa,* is a corruption of the Aztec *cacao.*) After the kernels (called nibs) are extracted from the bean, they're ground, and the grinding causes a marvellous liquid to flow—chocolate liquor, from which cocoa butter and cocoa powder are derived.

Thousands of years ago, the Olmec Indians of Mexico grew and harvested cocoa beans, and, in their turn, the Mayans cultivated cocoa plantations. The Mayans made a drink out of the chocolate liquor they produced. So did the Aztecs, who introduced the Spaniards to the drink. From two of the aboriginal languages in Mexico, the Spaniards coined the word *chocolate.* They took it home with them, and the conquest of Europe by chocolate was under way.

The flavour of chocolate blends very well with that of coffee, which has its own exotic history. The coffee tree originated in Ethiopia. According to a Yemeni legend, a shepherd saw his goats cropping reddish berries from a tree nearby. Curious when they grew restless and edgy after eating them, he plucked some berries himself and ate them. He too became animated. At the end of the day, the shepherd took berries back to his village, where the rest of the villagers tried them. They liked the effect, finding the berries kept them awake during prayers. Then the shepherd collected yet more berries and took them to a holy man, who ground them, boiled them, and discovered that he'd produced a bitter drink.

The rest really is history. In Yemen at the end of the thirteenth century, the drink acquired its name, *qahwah,* from which comes the word *coffee.* And Mocha, a Yemeni port, lent its name to the flavour that results from the combination of coffee and chocolate. (By the way, when coffee is used as a food flavouring, its caffeine content is negligible.)

Vanilla, chocolate, and coffee, all three building blocks of countless ice-cream recipes, all three travelling the trade routes to Europe at around the same time, heading straight for the coffee houses and cafés, from which the ice-cream parlour evolved.

You can still find the coffee house in the ice-cream parlour. There's something about the seating arrangement in both that encourages conversation. People sit opposite each other, almost knee to knee. They lean in so that word games can be played, confidences shared, and cases made. As tradition has it, the stage was set from early days by the Café Procope in Paris, with its small marble tables against a backdrop of large ornate mirrors and chande-liers. And even if ice cream wasn't served there when

Francesco Procopio dei Coltelli established the café in 1686 (opinion's divided), it certainly was as time passed and business flourished.

Situated close to the new theatre of the Comédie-Française, the Procope began to receive patrons who'd been to see a performance of Molière or Racine, and it developed into a place to discuss drama, literature, art, music. Or to argue politics, the obsession of café conversation. In the 1790s, it was recognized as a favourite spot for the revolutionaries. In part, the Procope became famous because of the people who were said to frequent it—Diderot, Benjamin Franklin, Voltaire, Robespierre, Danton, Marat, Napoleon, Georges Sand, Alfred de Musset, Anatole France, Verlaine, among others—who, in the beginning, came to drink coffee, chocolate, tea, lemonade, aromatic waters, liqueurs, and sweet wines, and later on were able to eat ice cream as well.

The word *café* in French means both the drink and the place. In the seventeenth century, coffee arrived in Europe from the Middle East, which also provided the model of a coffee house, a *café*. The Middle Eastern version was first described by Prospero Alpina of Padua, who visited Egypt in 1580. Coffee was enjoyed, he explained, "not during a meal, but afterwards ... while taking one's ease in the company of friends." In Italy the *caffè* provided just such an ambience—for example, the Caffè Greco in Rome, where Casanova, Keats, Byron, Goethe, Liszt, Wagner, and even the Mad King of Bavaria came to imbibe. Europeans ran with the idea of the coffee house while they happily became habituated to the drink.

For my money, something of the original ambience survives in the Viennese coffee house. You may find marble tables and crystal chandeliers. You will always find newspapers for reading. The Viennese coffee house claims to trace its origin back to 1683, when the Turkish army, in retreat from a siege of the city, left behind three hundred sacks that turned out to contain coffee beans. With them, an enterprising Pole named Franz Kolschitzky is said to have opened the first coffee house. It has even been suggested that Kolschitzky served iced coffee with whipped cream ("Viennese-style"), then turned it into an ice (ice cream). In her *History of Food,* Maguelonne Toussaint-Samat takes her suggestion even further, locating the Procope in Paris within the Viennese orbit of influence, claiming that its owner, Coltelli, was inspired to serve ices by Kolschitzky's example. Was he? If the devil's in the details, there are none. But ice cream did reach the precinct of the Paris café eventually.

As for the London coffee house, to which the likes of Samuel Pepys, Daniel Defoe, Jonathan Swift, and William Hogarth repaired, it never served ice cream as far as is known. London wasn't famous for its ice cream. That is, not until Robert Gunter, the son of one of the most influential of the London confectioners, James Gunter, went to Paris around 1815 to study at the illustrious Tortoni's, no less. When this native son returned, he made Gunter's synonymous with the best-quality ice cream, rivalling that in the rest of Europe.

Not surprisingly, the style of the French *café-glacier* was transplanted to English soil, as an 1820 scene by the artist John James Chalon demonstrates. It shows a little family sitting at a table, enjoying ice cream together. They aren't the only patrons. In the background, holding the pot high above the cup in the Middle Eastern manner, a waiter pours coffee for an older gentleman who's perusing a menu. Or perhaps he's reading a news periodical. To one side, a dandy lounges casually in a chair, licking an ice, while, at his feet, his dog begs for a taste. In the chair next to them, a child is cheerfully tucking into an ice with both hands. Since place dictates style as well as content, the civility that women and children require dominates the room. It's atmospheres away from the boisterous, smoke-filled London coffee house, where females were not welcome. The point is, the ice-cream parlour has improved everyone's manners.

FAMILY IN A LONDON "ICE CAFÉ"

By the 1830s, when the English naval hero Captain Frederick Marryat visited an ice-cream parlour in St. Louis, Missouri, he was shocked to see working men enter without their coats or waistcoats, their shirt sleeves rolled up, then proceed to sit down and order. But this was the American frontier, after all, and, soon enough, westerners got the hang of the situation. Ice cream was accepted as family entertainment, with all the civilizing effects that it entails.

Parfait—"perfect." According to the *Larousse Gastronomique,* it was originally a coffee-flavoured French ice dessert, made in a tall, thin mould, then unmoulded and presented in all its glory on a fancy plate. Parfaits were tremendously popular in the nineteenth century. In the North American version, vanilla ice cream, flavoured with liqueur or syrup of various kinds, including chocolate, whatever your fancy, is served in a tall, thin, footed parfait glass.

The date the parfait was introduced is lost in history, but it's a perfect treat for an old-fashioned ice-cream parlour to serve. The parfait glass is part of the act; you wouldn't get one in a modern ice-cream outlet, where the gleaming array of glasses, all of them descendants of goblets à glace, have been replaced by waxed cardboard cups. To enjoy a parfait in a glass, take yourself to a vintage parlour or, at the very least, seek out a facsimile—say, the ice-cream parlour that Walt Disney inaugurated in Disneyland, California, in 1955, or its counterpart in Disney World, Florida, which opened in 1971. The elegant ice-cream parlour is now a recreation, as interested in illusion as in ice cream.

There's one other place you might find one, though it too is either a relic or a recreation: the old-time drugstore soda fountain. The soda fountain joined the work that the ice-cream parlour had begun, operating side by side with it. That's how it was conceived from the start, as a further example of the civilizing effects of ice cream and a distinctly American contribution to the ideal of good clean family fun. The look of the soda fountain, however, and its special theatrics are another matter entirely, related to the importance of soda water over coffee. The appeal of technology produced its own flamboyant aesthetics, and the show began back in an era in the United States when ice cream teamed up with soda water.

Visualize the soda fountain itself, as it was in the early part of the nineteenth century. Water infused with carbonic-acid gas was generated in a labyrinthine apparatus of chambers, pipes, and reservoirs, usually found in the basement of the drugstore, and stored in a graceful urn set on marble columns above the counter upstairs. But the classical decorum was deceptive. Sometimes, belowstairs, the generator exploded. And frequently, when the spigot on the urn was opened, the soda water hissed, gurgled, spit—and doused whatever and whoever lay in its path. To appreciate the risk, all you have to do is think of the pressure build-up behind the cap of a single bottle of soda water. In due course, the right pressure cock was installed, and mechanical problems were solved.

By 1858, the urn had been replaced by a rectangular fountain. One model, with a marble-topped counter, contained the soda water, multiple spigots, a device for delivering shaved ice, and, of course, containers for the many syrups as well: vanilla, lemon, strawberry, raspberry, grenadine, apple, mulberry, peach, and sarsaparilla were among a host of flavours that went into the soda water. The number of flavours grew as the century progressed, and the fountain showed off its versatility in drink after flavoured, carbonated drink. There were medicinal sodas too—bicarbonate of soda, bromo-caffeine, tincture ginger, quinine. After all, the soda fountain owed its existence to a long line of druggist-inventors, -manufacturers, and -artists.

Over time, the aesthetics became operatic in scope. James W. Tufts, originally a druggist from a small town near Boston, built a successful firm under the name Arctic Soda. Tufts was the greatest soda-fountain showman of them all. Like St. Paul on the road to Damascus, he converted—in his case, to the vocation of designer. Or rather, he established the right conditions for the many designers he hired. They built a fountain that looked like a cabin (it was also referred to as a doghouse), a French cottage with a vase of flowers on its roof. Soon they upped the ante to a castle. Designers in other firms hurried to follow suit. Fountains became temples, tombs, embellished with statuary gargoyles, sphinxes, knights, and nymphs.

But Tufts succeeded in outdoing all his competitors. At the Centennial Exhibition, held in Philadelphia in 1876 to mark the one-hundredth anniversary of the Declaration of Independence, he introduced his firm's masterwork. People would not have believed it if they hadn't seen it with their own eyes—a marble soda fountain that rose 33 feet in the air and weighed 30 tons. It was adorned with columns, clocks, even vases to hold flowers. In a swelteringly hot July in Philadelphia, crowds thronged to Tufts's fountain to quench their thirst. And here's where ice-cream sodas made their entrance. They were just a few years old, the latest craze, when James W. Tufts paid $50,000 for the sole right of dispensing them from his spectacular marble edifice at the exhibition.

Over the following decades, soda fountains became simpler in design. They had to—who could compete with

ICE CREAM

JAMES W. TUFTS'S SODA FOUNTAIN AT THE
CENTENNIAL EXHIBITION IN PHILADELPHIA IN 1876

Tufts's folly? But they still featured paraphernalia enough to create an impression: marble counters, bent-iron chairs, metal glass holders of all shapes and sizes. And, of course, there was the soda itself. A little flavoured syrup or fruit in syrup, soda water from the fountain to fill the glass three-quarters full, followed by two scoops of ice cream and an additional squirt of soda water, all of these ingredients topped with whipped cream and, depending on how you feel about it, a maraschino cherry. The soda itself is straightforward enough. But the story of its invention in those heady days is anything but.

There are several claimants to the title of inventor, and the narrative follows the old, familiar pattern in the annals of ice cream: innovation results from improvisation. Robert Green of Philadelphia, for example, claimed that, in 1874, at his stand selling soda-fountain drinks, he ran out of cream. The moment he decided to substitute vanilla ice cream, the soda was born. He'd intended to let the ice cream melt, Green explained, but customers were impatiently waiting. Fred Sanders of Detroit insisted he had the lucky accident first. (Alas for Sanders, the date of his eureka moment was not recorded.) On a hot day, all the cream in his drugstore soured, so he improvised with some fruit syrup, adding a scoop of ice cream and pouring soda water on top. That leaves two newsboys from New York City in the running, and they were careful about chronology. (Alas for them, their *names* were never recorded.) The boys said that, in 1872, in a sweet shop they frequented, with the permission of the owner they added a slice of pineapple to a glass of ice cream, then poured in the soda water. On another occasion, they experimented with ginger ale over ice cream. The shop's owner was said to have gone on to perfect the drink, but his name, too, was never recorded.

Robert Green wasn't about to surrender his turf. He fought back, specifying that the inscription on his tombstone should read: "The Originator of the Ice-cream Soda." At his death in 1920, he got his wish.

"Black and white"—a chocolate soda with vanilla ice cream. "Black stick"—a chocolate ice-cream cone. This is the jargon of the soda jerk. It probably began in the nineteenth century and developed into a singularly imaginative language as time went by. "Eighty-one"—a glass of water. "Eighty-seven and a half"—an attractive woman is approaching. "Ninety-five" or "white bread"—the boss is on his way. Because the customer couldn't translate what was being said, it was code, cheeky and fun. "Belch water"—a glass of seltzer.

Fortunately, the language caught the attention of the likes of H. L. Mencken and other, lesser-known but scrupulous scholars who wrote it down, preserving it even as it was dying out. "Mug of murk," "draw one," "leg off a pair of drawers," "in the dark," "midnight," "no cow"— all epithets for a cup of black coffee. From the beginning of the twentieth century until the 1930s, this way of speaking was one of the attractions of the soda jerk (so named because he—always a he—jerked the draft arm on the fountain to release the soda water). The jerk was fluent in expressing himself in his work and celebrated for his performance. "Bucket of hail"—small glass of ice.

Imagine you have one in front of you now, as you sit, a customer at a soda fountain that has perfected its functional shape. It's a free-standing counter, streamlined and ready for action, with the requisite draft arms, syrups, pumps, and deep wells for ice cream installed in it. And standing behind the counter is the soda jerk, who wants to know what'll it be.

Chocolate soda, you specify.

You watch him draw the chocolate syrup into the glass, fill it three-quarters full with soda water, tipping the glass so that he avoids splashing, revolving it so that he blends the water and syrup thoroughly. Every move he makes is as choreographed as a dance. He's careful with the last squirt. It mustn't strike the one scoop of ice cream he's added so far, or else it will fragment. A fine stream will do the trick. Very gently, he slides in the second scoop, so that it will float and make an effect when he hands the soda over the counter. So there's your "choc in."

Though I'm taking poetic licence here, there *were* such instructions for soda jerks. This choreography is taken from the *Ice Cream Review* of September 1940. The writer, C. E. Henderson, also noted that being behind the counter was comparable to being in a show window, to being an artist demonstrating the right way to mix the perfect chocolate ice-cream soda. But humour me. Imagine instead that it's May 5, 1923, in Fred Robertson's Drugstore, in Dayton, Tennessee.

As you "suck" your soda, opposite you at one of the tables is a young biology teacher, John Scopes. He often comes to the drugstore for an ice-cream soda. You can see him in the large mirror behind the counter, and you can hear everything too. He's sitting with a local businessman and a school superintendent, and they're in animated conversation.

"Would you be willing to stand for a test case?" the businessman asks.

It's the moment when Scopes is being persuaded to go to court and fight for the right to teach Darwin's theory of evolution in a Tennessee classroom. "The best time to scotch the snake is when it starts to wiggle," he will say when he looks back on the case. Right now, drawing on his straw, he's silent for a moment. And then, he agrees.

John Scopes himself described the meeting in Robertson's that day. And when the trial was over, the drugstore was proud to advertise itself as the place where "the Monkey Trial" began, letting it be known that not only Scopes but Clarence Darrow, who defended the case, and Mencken, who covered it, were regular customers. Robertson's Drugstore put up signs on the roads leading into town and sold souvenirs on the premises.

In short, in every city and small town in North America, the drugstore soda fountain provided a meeting place. It had its extraordinary and ordinary days, its fictional days too. In Thornton Wilder's play *Our Town,* the teenagers George Gibbs and Emily Webb work out their relationship in Mr. Morgan's drugstore in Grover's Corners. As they sip strawberry sodas together, they realize they're falling in love. The fountain was an accepted trysting spot, and more.

Prohibition offered a reason to expand. In the 1920s and '30s, New York City boasted an 800-seat and Chicago a 1,200-seat fountain. Countless sodas were made for lovers, lawyers, teachers, politicians—teetotallers, every one. Legend has it that Lana Turner was discovered at the soda-fountain counter at Schwab's Drugstore, at the corner of Hollywood and Vine. Paramount had a reproduction of it on the backlot because it was featured in so many scripts. Without Schwab's, the history of American movies wouldn't be the same.

In the 1950s, the advent of the car, the suburbs, and the supermarket helped kill off the soda fountain. The corner drugstore was replaced by the mall. People bought their ice cream at the supermarket, took it home and made sodas in the rec room. As I write this, the Ice Screamers, about eight hundred collectors of ice-cream memorabilia, have just wrapped up their annual convention. Every June they meet in Lancaster, Pennsylvania, and they've done so ever since they were founded in 1980, by Ed Marks. Some of them were soda jerks when they were young. (So, too, were Bob Hope, Jerry Lewis, Jack Kerouac, Malcolm X, and Duke Ellington, whose first composition was "The Soda Fountain Rag.") At their conventions, they put on tastings, hold an auction, and host lectures. They display ice-cream stools, dippers, postcards, old signs, straw holders, mixers, freezers, glassware, even Dixie cup lids. They buy, sell, trade and socialize, and they publish a quarterly newsletter. They're antiquarians.

....

BLACK COW SODA (1944)

Root beer syrup
Ice cream, or whipped cream, or coffee cream
Vanilla ice cream
Carbonated water
Whipped cream

Into a soda glass put 1 1/2 ounces root beer syrup. Add 1 soda spoon whipped cream or ice cream or 1 1/2 coffee cream, and blend. Add fine stream carbonated water until the glass is 3/4 full. Float into the carbonated mixture 2 No. 24 dippers vanilla ice cream. If glass is not full, finish filling with coarse stream carbonated water. Top with whipped cream.

....

Ice-cream parlours may not be as refined as they used to be, but they're still very jolly. After a slump in the 1950s, they began to be popular again in the '60s. The

Italians especially have made them pop with living colour just as they do back in Italy. My friends and I have moved on to a gelateria with bright tiles, intense paint on the walls, and vats lined up, shoulder to shoulder, in a glass case for viewing. The game is still afoot. The topic now is a film script involving ice cream, and we decide on an Italian plot.

"How about one involving Viagra ice cream?" Greg says. "It seems to be gaining in popularity in Italy, with women too."

So we mull it over. The ice cream is blue, and that's amusing. But who knows whether the blue represents the real stuff?

Gilbert, who draws inspiration from a sensuous Italian setting, has another idea. "We might adopt something from Fellini's short film *Bevete più Latte*. It's about a very repressed bachelor who lives in a little apartment on the outskirts of Rome. He's ready to go to sleep but hears this little jingle outside his window, 'Da-da-da-dadada, *bevete più latte*.' It goes away, and then he hears it again. He goes to the window, pulls open the shutters and looks out. And there's a huge billboard which shows Anita Ekberg, lying flat, like an odalisque. Her most spectacular assets are aimed at his window, so to speak. And this little refrain starts again, 'Da-da-da-dadada, *bevete più latte.*' Slowly, he begins to fall in love with this huge billboard."

"What's that got to do with ice cream?" I want to know.

"Milk makes ice cream," Gilbert explains patiently.

"*Mangia gelato, mangia gelato,*" Greg sings. "And what size are Anita's 'most spectacular assets'? Two cups. We're back to Freud again."

"I guess," Gilbert admits, "subconsciously, I was focusing on the two cups."

We don't know it at that moment, but the association between mother's milk and ice cream has already been made, by the author of *Everything You Always Wanted to Know About Sex but Were Afraid to Ask*. In 1971, David Reuben told a women's magazine that milk rules the subconscious mind of men, that women enter into that mind as the providers of milk, that ice cream reminds them of Oedipal urges that lie within.

I offer in evidence a final signature piece, a famous ice-cream dish named for yet another celebrity. It was created by Oscar Tschirky—Oscar of New York's Waldorf-Astoria hotel in the Gilded Age of the 1890s. In this instance, he was honouring Lillian Russell, a singer and actress billed as "the American beauty." She loved to eat, and she was buxom. One evening, Russell's "friend," Diamond Jim Brady, brought her into the hotel for dinner. Buttressed in a corset that trimmed her waist and emphasized her "spectacular assets," she sat there, unable to decide whether to order ice cream or melon. Oscar leapt to the challenge. His dish, the "Lillian Russell," may have been simple, but it was highly symbolic. The chef just filled half a cantaloupe with ice cream. Now, what does that remind you of? Da-da-da-dadada …

You never know where the show business of ice cream will lead you.

EPILOGUE

THE GOOD LIFE

You've read this far so you already know: the good life is one with ice cream in it, beginning in childhood and continuing unabated into old age. Amen to that possibility. Ice cream is associated with good times and family, loving friends and special places, and here's a charming vignette that illustrates the point.

In 1803, Eliza Bowne, a young lady of marriageable age, was visiting New York City. At the time, pleasure gardens were in vogue—a lovely name for what was simply a commercial outdoor entertainment complex. Eliza wrote her friend Octavia Southgate that, accompanied by her hosts, she'd gone to a pleasure garden in "the cool of the evening." While she listened to music, Eliza enjoyed a lemonade and an ice and departed "happy and refreshed." We wouldn't know anything about her little outing if her letters had not been collected in a book called *A Girl's Life Eighty Years Ago,* published in 1887, long after Eliza's death. For her, the visit to the pleasure garden was just a satisfying moment during her trip to the city. There must be thousands upon thousands of such moments that feature ice cream and remain unknown, anonymous.

When I began thinking about the subject of ice cream, I imagined an impersonal, encompassing history. It is there, of course. But, as I went along, I discovered this fabric of personal accounts containing their own particular truth. Sometimes they have a plot; sometimes they're merely a scene. But they branch and flower like the strands in a medieval romance and still make up a unity. Wherever ice cream is found, it immediately assumes a local complexion, and local meanings are attached to it. But the best ice-cream stories translate the particular into the universal, and everyone can feel included. The good life's a full life.

The stories of my friends fell into my lap. Ice cream is a part of so many people's memories. Soon I began soliciting stories too. It may be interesting to note that ice cream can be frozen to $-40°C$, vacuum-dried and sealed in a foil packet, as was done for the astronauts on the Apollo space missions. Or that it can be frozen by liquid nitrogen into small round beads, which Curt Jones of Lexington, Kentucky, is selling right now under the brand name Dippin' Dots. Both examples prove that the popularity of the dessert knows no bounds—especially given that Jones discovered how to deep-freeze ice cream while working in cryogenics, researching the commercial preservation of bacteria and enzymes. But these examples are merely curiosities. Associations, on the other hand, take time to grow.

In Thornton Wilder's play *The Skin of Our Teeth,* the maid, Sabina, says: "My advice to you is not to inquire into why or whither, but just enjoy your ice cream while it's on your plate—that's my philosophy." Of course, the characters in *The Skin of Our Teeth* are facing an imminent Ice Age and the end of the world. Since they can't prevent the apocalypse, they might as well enjoy the ice cream. Sabina's advice is particularly fitting. "Gather ye rosebuds while ye may" is how the seventeenth-century poet Robert Herrick put it.

But I submit that, while children can focus exclusively on the present, adults find that difficult to do. Too much experience and recollection bars the way. So memories of time past are the stuff from which these stories are made. I'm going to offer a farewell sampling of them, remind you of some history as well as literature and art, and dub the entire result "The Ice-cream Chronicles."

Audrey Wright's voice on the telephone is warm and friendly. I don't know her personally, but she has heard I've been looking for ice-cream stories, and she wants to tell me hers.

"In the 1960s, we were students attending a university in west Texas, and we were married," she says, referring to her husband, Blenus Wright. "We used to get together with other couples every Sunday night, and we'd have ice-cream parties." She laughs. "In July and August, it was very hot in west Texas. I could probably fantasize that we had them every week in the summer."

"Sort of ice-cream socials," I say.

"That's right. Maybe there were six to eight couples, and each couple chose a different flavour to bring—that was pre-arranged. One couple had an electric ice-cream maker, but several of us hand-churned our ice cream."

As she talks, I'm wondering whether there was a conscious appeal to an earlier, simpler time. The 1960s were turbulent. All Audrey says is that it was cheaper to make ice cream that way; they were students.

"Do you still hand-churn ice cream?" I ask her.

"No, we go out and buy it from the local truck," she says, then pauses. "I just realized something. Those ice-cream parties in Texas remind me of summers when I was a child. We'd spend two weeks' vacation in the small town of Arnstein in northern Ontario, where we'd go to visit my father's family. Sunday afternoon, the whole family would gather under the big pine trees near the old frame house. It was the men's job to churn the ice cream, while the women were busy getting the bowls. It was always vanilla."

It's this traditional scene of ice-cream making that speaks so strongly to our sense of human community. Until there was steam, followed by electric freezers, pasteurizers, packaging machines, refrigerated railway cars and delivery vans, until ice cream was mass produced, in other words, it was an intimate affair, involving sisters, brothers, cousins, aunts and uncles, grandparents, parents, and friends. Everyone came together. The dasher had to be turned constantly until the ice cream was ready. In a sense, every batch of homemade ice cream was an authored piece, a personalized creation; automation rendered ice cream anonymous.

And the transition was rapid. In the early days of ice-cream factories, people worked large hand-cranked freezers. William Neilson, who opened a plant in Toronto, Ontario, bought three used ones—all he could afford on a shoestring budget. In 1893, the first year of production in his plant, Neilson, his wife, and their five children hand-cranked some 3,750 gallons. Neilson's strapping son, Morden, was required to churn faster as the ice-cream mixture froze. Soon, though, horses hitched to treadmills kept the crank turning by means of a system of pulleys, belts, and levers. By 1900, the horses were gone, and steam boilers and gasoline engines had arrived. In 1905, the first commercial batch freezer was invented (producing one batch at a time, that is). By 1926, the continuous freezer was up and running. In just a few decades, the ice-cream factory had become streamlined, efficient, modern.

In the 1920s, Americans were introducing ice cream to China, exporting complete soda fountains to Japan and Chile, sailing across the Atlantic to teach high-powered production techniques to Europeans. There was ice cream on airplanes. Just think: all that industrialization is ignored when you churn ice cream by hand. You invoke a past that's local, prior, earth-bound, static (by comparison), and communal. No wonder nostalgia is a theme in so many ice-cream stories.

LEARNING TO MANAGE AN ICE-CREAM CONE

I pull out a photograph that was sent to me by one of my dearest friends, Frances Wainwright. It shows her as a little girl of three, wide-eyed, holding a cone, trying to prevent the ice cream from dripping down onto her clothes. Her expression is wide-eyed with the endeavour. The problem is, the ice cream has already dripped over her hand and the cone and is slipping relentlessly downwards, as melting ice cream is wont to do. Ice cream from the point of view of a child—or is it? I see in the photograph a perfect allegory for the inevitable passage of time, and that's the kind of pensive speculation only a grown-up would indulge in. The child is too busy trying to manage the cone.

Adults eat more ice cream than children, and more than half of it is in the form of ice-cream cones. It's natural the cones should be remembered. But the photograph of my friend as a little girl was taken by an adult aware of mutability. There's a second or two when all of us think: record this memory, this snapshot when time seemed to stand still. We get in the habit of freeze-framing. Frances and I once enjoyed tartufo together in the Piazza Navona in Rome. Chocolate ice cream covered with bittersweet chocolate, cherries, and whipped cream, named after the truffle because of its shape, tartufo is a Roman specialty.

We sat at a table outside Tre Scalini, the café where it originated in 1946, and spoke of her parents, who had come to this café to enjoy it many years before us. In fact, Frances promised her mother she'd eat ice cream in the Piazza Navona and think of them. In a sense, we were building our memory onto theirs. Now, whenever I order tartufo, wherever I am, a picture of Rome comes immediately to mind—the day, the light, the two fountains in the exquisite square, and my friend and me deep in conversation.

Recently, I asked her son, Julian, who is living and working in Hanoi, Vietnam, what he knew about ice cream in that country. He explained that the Vietnamese word for ice cream is *kem,* that it likely derives from the French *crème,* that, along with sorbets of Vietnamese flavours—durian, mango, young rice, and coconut—he could also get *kem caramen,* or crème caramel, because the popularity of ice cream in Vietnam, he believed, is a direct outcome of the French colonial period. He followed his explanation with a personal memory: "In Hanoi, in the summertime, the streets that have ice-cream parlours are clogged with traffic, as families go out in the evenings to eat the stuff—three or four people on a motorbike, eating rapidly melting vanilla in the stifling heat. The sidewalks society to which he belonged, and to which I'd been invited to speak about the meaning of ice cream. A small, alert, no-nonsense man, he was sitting in the front row beside his wife, Janka. When I solicited stories from the audience, briefly, he told his. I noticed he spoke with a slight accent. Afterwards, I telephoned him and gathered more details. Stan Seydegart was in his eighties. He was Polish, born in Warsaw. In 1941, when Hitler and Stalin agreed to divide the country and his part of it was occupied by the Nazis, he decided to get out.

At twenty-two, he found himself, relying on fake papers, trying to get to Japan by going east, travelling by train all the way to Moscow. And there, to his surprise, he found ice cream. "In every station of the subway," he said, "they were selling cheap ice-cream cones. There was chocolate and vanilla, I remember. They called it *moroschnije*." Stan Seydegart lined up with the Russians to buy it. Because of his different clothes, he stood out as an outsider. But he was treated well, even pushed to the front of the line. "There was very little food around," he told me, repeating what he'd said at the meeting. "Isn't it odd? Isn't it odd? There was ice cream."

Moroschnije is simply the Russian word for "ice cream." In the nineteenth century, street vendors in St. Petersburg

used to call out, *"Moroschnije ssami ssladkija moroschnije!"*—
"Ice, the sweetest ice in the world!" During the Soviet
Union, ice cream was sweet, cheap, and exceptionally
good—as it had been since 1926, when Anastas Mikoyan
was appointed minister of trade. Mikoyan turned his
attention to dairy co-operatives and set up the Moscow
ice-cream factory, making the treat available to the
proletariat. Even though the ice cream was factory
produced, it contained no artificial additives and was
made with fresh eggs and cream. After the collapse of
communism, Western brands entered Russia, and, though
a large, indigenous industry still supplies most of the
market, the quality isn't what it used to be.

Stan Seydegart never got over finding ice cream in a
subway station in a city on the brink of disaster. You see,
this story took place just before the German invasion of
Moscow, when terrible deprivation ensued. I wonder
what the ice cream meant to the Russians in the queue
with him that day. Perhaps *moroschnije,* because of its
familiarity, offered them some reassurance that their
home was safe, at least for the moment. Often ice cream
has been a comforting reminder of home. During World
War II, U.S. newspapers printed such headlines as
"Soldier Dreams of Whole Mountain of Ice Cream" (the

Memphis *Press Scimitar*) and "South Pacific Wounded Want Ice Cream First" (the St. Louis *Globe-Democrat*).

There is an even more powerful example of this attempt at rootedness. An American in a Japanese POW camp was barely existing on a starvation diet when he dreamed up a Thanksgiving Day menu including all the foods he missed: turkey, ham, rabbit, giblet gravy, cranberry sauce, sweet potatoes, peas, string beans, olives, pickles, salad, fruit, apple pie, pumpkin pie—and that's only a sampling of his enormous menu. Then, just before the coffee, cigarettes, beer, and cigars that signalled the end of the meal, he jotted down, "Assorted Ice Cream." Army Mess Sergeant Morris Lewis kept that menu, celebrating everything about home that he could find represented in its holiday fare. Plenty, communality, kinship. He might have cheered himself up much as Charles Dickens did with obsessive food recitations in his novels. Perhaps if paper and pen had been less precious, Lewis might have gone on to write a story surrounding a feast that was more than Dickensian in abundance. Would there be jokes and toasts? Would the men in the mess fall asleep after dinner? Would they polish off their ice cream and ask for more? As food for the soul, ice cream has been shaped by the imagination, and imagining could hold Lewis together until he was released.

Eventually the narrator realizes that it isn't the taste of the madeleine that thrills him but his own success in retrieving the contents of his memories. His voluntary, as opposed to involuntary, retrieval. His imagination playing on the past.

At a gathering of old friends at the end of this missive, the narrator finds himself trying to jibe what he recollects of events with the versions of others. Proust has devoted fifteen years of his life to writing about memory, only to discover that it is always about the struggle for identity. From occurrence to occurrence, from moment to moment, each one of us is engaged in writing a life story in our heads. In this respect, ice cream is as potent a cue as a madeleine. But, to become a part of who we are, ice cream, like the madeleine, must be intensely experienced the first time around.

If what sticks in the memory is personality, colour, incident, accident, all of that is banished from the commercial making and distribution of ice cream. I've already said that automation renders it anonymous. In the largest operations, the "product" moves from machine to machine through automated stages controlled by computer. There need be no intervention by human hand until lids are put on the containers—and in some plants, machines even do that too. The formula for the ice cream remains rigorously the same, dictated at a distance.

And there's no space more undifferentiated than a supermarket freezer. Beyond the grouping of brand name after brand name, there's no ordering that signifies narrative. Ice cream is next to sherbet. Chocolate-covered ice-cream bars lie down with frozen yogurt. You'd never know that epic battles had been won and lost here—that, during the 1950s, when people began to buy ice cream from supermarkets, thousands of small plants were fighting for freezer space and many of them went down to defeat.

But in the 1960s the tide turned. Alongside the giants and their franchises, a cottage industry sprang up, and individually owned gelaterias, scoop shops, and stands boasted ice cream made on the premises. What the proliferation of small businesses proves is that people were missing not simply taste but context, and they succeeded, to a degree, in getting them back. Some of the original intimacy of making ice cream has returned.

It's even possible nowadays to be involved over the counter. "Slabberies" have come into existence, where ice cream is mixed in plain view on a marble or granite slab—hence the name—and you get to choose the candy bits, cookies, brownies, fruits, nuts, and sauces that go into it yourself. Well, in ice-cream stories too, it's what you do with the elements that counts.

When I travel, I always make a point of having ice cream in whatever city or town I'm visiting. At a stand or a café, I join everybody else who's indulging in it too, perhaps order a cone and join the community of strollers in the streets nearby. We're a living tableau of a shared past. At any point, we can enter that past imaginatively, and connections with the present are revealed. The proof is in the eating.

During the unusual winter of 1793–94, Beethoven noted in a letter: "The Viennese are afraid it will soon be impossible to have any ice cream, for, as the winter is mild, ice is rare." Obviously, in Vienna, they believed that ice cream was a treat for all seasons. And apparently we've continued to smudge the boundaries between winter and summer when it comes to ice cream. May Appleyard, who came to Canada from England in 1911, reminisced for CBC Radio about her stop in Winnipeg: "We went into Eaton's [department store] … and what got me was the people who were eating ice cream when it was freezing outside."

In the *Tatler* newspaper of March 18–21, 1709, Joseph Addison attacked the gourmet pretensions of his fellow Londoners. He'd attended a dinner party where the guests, as he said, were "cooling their Mouths with Lumps of Ice." Addison was mocking the "ices" that were served as part of a French-style dessert; he didn't entirely approve of French desserts, particularly when a good plain English one would do. But it's no surprise that his satire fell on deaf ears. Ice cream crossed national boundaries then, as it has continued to do ever since. French ice cream was served to first-class passengers on board the *Titanic*. Second-class passengers had to settle for the eggless sort, as a menu that survives from April 14, 1912, makes clear. This story also demonstrates how ice cream can be used for purposes other than edible ones.

"We dare not trust our wit for making our house pleasant to our friend, so we buy ice creams," Ralph Waldo Emerson scoffed in his lecture "Man the Reformer" in 1841. What can we have in mind when we extend this frozen dish to our pets? The market is there. Ananova, a Belgian company, is selling Dog Ice, in the shape of a big bone, low in sugar and carbohydrates. CoolBrands, the

Canadian firm, has its cups and cakes under the Dogster label, offering such flavours as Nutly (peanut butter and cheese) and United Fido Orbiters (oat cookies and cheese). I ask everyone I know, "Have you ever heard of ice cream for dogs?" and am greeted with a chorus of "What?" I think it's only when we're startled into considering doggy ice cream that we realize how entrenched our commitment to this confection is, how willing we are to be witless about it.

A wild orchid grows in the mountains of southeastern Turkey, and its root supplies *salep,* from which ice cream is made in the Middle East. According to a BBC News story from 2003, this orchid is in danger of extinction. Shepherds who collect it for the ice cream report that the plant is disappearing and that they have to climb higher and higher into the mountains in pursuit of it. Right now, *salep* has been prohibited for export, and environmentalists are urging a complete ban on its use. In the ice-cream capital of Marash, however, Mehmet Kumble doesn't plan to cut back on production. He maintains that ice cream has been made with *salep* in Turkey since the time of the Ottoman rulers, who believed the root was an aphrodisiac because it looks like a testicle. (That's what the word *salep* means. So does *orchis,* the Greek word for "orchid.") Mehmet Kumble's factory uses up to three tons of *salep,*

SELECT BIBLIOGRAPHY

PRIMARY SOURCES

Arbuckle, W. S. *Ice Cream*. Fourth edition. Westport: AVI Publishing., 1986.

Arnold, Shannon Jackson. *Everybody Loves Ice Cream: The Whole Scoop on America's Favorite Treat*. Cincinnati: Emmis Books, 2004.

Courtine, Robert J. *Larousse Gastronomique*. Paris: Larousse, 1984.

Cox, J. Stevens. *Ice-creams of Queen Victoria's Reign*. Guernsey: Toucan Press, 1970.

David, Elizabeth. *The Harvest of the Cold Months: The Social History of Ice and Ices*. London: Michael Joseph, 1994.

Davidson, Alan, ed. *The Penguin Companion to Food*. London: Penguin Books, 2002.

Dickson, Paul. *The Great American Ice Cream Book*. New York: Atheneum, 1978.

Funderburg, Anne Cooper. *Sundae Best: A History of Soda Fountains*. Madison: University of Wisconsin Press, 2003.

———. *Chocolate, Strawberry, and Vanilla: A History of American Ice Cream*. Bowling Green, OH: Bowling Green State University Popular Press, 1995.

Lidell, Caroline, and Robin Weir. *Frozen Desserts: The Definitive Guide to Making Ice Creams, Ices, Sorbets, Gelati, and Other Frozen Delights*. New York: St. Martin's Griffin, 1996.

Marshall, Mrs. A. B. *Ices Plain and Fancy*. Introduction and annotation by Barbara Ketcham Wheaton. New York: Metropolitan Museum of Art, 1976.

Marshall, Robert T., H. Douglas Goff, and Richard W. Hartel. *Ice Cream*. Sixth edition. New York: Kluwer Academic/Plenum Publishers, 2003.

McGee, Harold. *On Food and Cooking: The Science and Lore of the Kitchen*. New York: Charles Scribner's Sons, 1984.

Steingarten, Jeffrey. "The Mother of All Ice Cream" In his *The Man Who Ate Everything*. New York: Vintage Books, 1997.

Toussaint-Samat, Maguelonne. *History of Food*. Translated by Anthea Bell. Oxford: Blackwell Publishing, 1992.

Turback, Michael. *The Banana Split Book: Everything There Is to Know about America's Greatest Dessert*. Philadelphia: Camino Books, 2004.

Visser, Margaret. "Ice Cream: Cold Comfort." In her *Much Depends on Dinner*. Toronto: Harper Perennial Canada, 1991.

Wardlaw, Lee. *We All Scream for Ice Cream*. New York: HarperCollins, 2000.

Weinstein, Bruce. The Ultimate Ice Cream Book. New York: Morrow Cookbooks, 1999.

OTHER SOURCES

Appleyard, May. Interviewed on "Voice of the Pioneer," CBC Radio, May 17, 1979.

Ben and Jerry's. <http://www.benjerry.com/>. (Accessed August 17, 2004.)

Bowne, Eliza S. *A Girl's Life Eighty Years Ago: Selections from the Letters of Eliza Southgate Bowne.* New York: Charles Scribner's & Sons, 1887.

Brillat-Savarin, Jean-Anthelme. *The Physiology of Taste.* Translated by Anne Drayton. London: Penguin Books, 1994.

Fernandez-Armesto, Felipe. *Near a Thousand Tables.* Toronto: Key Porter Books, 2002.

"Food Timeline—History Notes: Ice Cream." <http://www.food timeline.org/foodicecream.html>. (Accessed July 1, 2004.)

Goffe, Douglas. "Ice Cream History and Folklore." <http://www.foodsci.uoguelph.ca/dairyedu/ichist.html>. (Accessed October 27, 2004.)

Grantham, Bill. "Brilliant Mischief: The French on Anti-Americanism." *World Policy Journal.* Volume XX, no. 2 (Summer, 2003). <http://worldpolicy.org/journal/articles/wpj03-2/grantham.html>. (Accessed July 6, 2004.)

Harrison, John. Interviewed by Michael Enright, *As It Happens,* CBC Radio One, July 10, 1991.

"History of Ice Cream in Philadelphia." <http://www.chilly philly.com/icehist.html>. (Accessed June 27, 2004.)

"The History of the Soda Fountain." <http://inventors.about.com/library/inventors/blsodafountain.htm>. (Accessed July 25, 2004.)

"Ice Scream Threatens Turkey's Flowers." BBC News, World Edition, August 5, 2003. <http://news.bbc.co.uk/2/hi/science/nature/3126047.stm>. (Accessed September 3, 2004.)

Ice Screamers. "Collecting Soda Fountain Memories." <http://www.icescreamers.com/>. (Accessed October 15, 2004.)

Jefferson, Thomas. "Thomas Jefferson's vanilla ice cream recipe." <http://www.loc.gov/exhibits/treasures/images/uc004810.jpg>. (Accessed June 23, 2004.)

Kaplow, Larry. "Ice Cream Is Sweet Solace to Iraqi People." *Detroit Free Press,* June 12, 2002. <http://www.freep.com/news/nw/niraq12_20020612.htm>. (Accessed July 10, 2004.)

Kurlansky, Mark. *Salt: A World History.* Toronto: Alfred A. Knopf Canada, 2002.

Lee, Matt, and Ted Lee. "Land of 1,000 Vanillas." *The New York Times Magazine,* October 31, 2004.

Lucas, Fiona. "Spadina's Magnificent Eureka Refrigerator." *The Old Toronto Advocate,* No. 6 (Summer 2004).

Marlowe, Jack. "Zalabia and the First Ice Cream Cone." *Saudi Aramco World* (July/August 2003).

Marryat, Frederick. *Diary in America.* Bloomington: Indiana University Press, 1960.

Martin, Chuck. "The Great Banana Split." *Cincinatti Enquirer,* June 3, 2001. <http://www.enquirer.com/editions/2001/06/03/tem_the_great_banana.html>. (Accessed July 29, 2004.)

McCarthy, Rory. "Inside the ice cream factory paralysed by import bans." *Guardian Unlimited.* <http://www.guardian.co.uk/international/story/0,3604,863259,00.html>. (Accessed July 10, 2004.)

McKee, Francis. "Home Back." <http://www.francismckee.com/ice.htm>. (Accessed February 4, 2001.)

Mitchell, Jared. "Cold War." *National Post Business,* January 2004.

Ranhofer, Charles. *The Epicurean: A Complete Treatise of the Analytical and Practical Studies of the Culinary Art.* New York: Dover, 1971.

Root, Waverley, and Richard de Rochemont. *Eating in America: A History.* New York: William Morrow, 1976.

Scott, Amy. "The Coldest Crop: Ice Harvesting in 19th and Early 20th Century Ontario." *The Old Toronto Advocate,* No. 5 (Winter 2004).

Slater, Nigel. *Toast: The Story of a Boy's Hunger.* New York: Penguin, 2004.

Sokolov, Raymond. "Semi-solid State Physics: A Feel for Ice cream." *Oxford Symposium on Food and Cookery 1993: Look and Feel.* London: Prospect Books, 1993.

Stradley, Linda. "History and Legends of Baked Alaska." <http://whatscookingamerica.net/History/IceCream/BakedAlaska.htm>. (Accessed July 7, 2004.)

———. "History of Ice Cream Sundae." <http://whatscooking america.net/History/IceCream/Sundae.htm>. (Accessed June 7, 2004.)

———. "History of the Ice Cream Cone." <http://whats cookingamerica.net/History/IceCream/IceCreamCone.htm>. (Accessed May 19, 2004.)

Thompson, Jan. "Prisoners of the Rising Sun: Food Memories of American POWs in the Far East During World War II." Paper presented to the Oxford Symposium on Food and Cookery, "Food and Memory," 2000.

"Totally Tot-Able Ice Cream Maker." <http://www.wasatch recreation.com/files/>. (Accessed December 9, 2004.)

ACKNOWLEDGMENTS

Only when a book is finished does it become obvious just how much help has been given along the way. It's a cumulative gift. I look back now and remember with gratitude those who listened, advised, encouraged, and always believed that the story of ice cream was worth the telling.

First and foremost, thanks are due to my editor at Penguin, Susan Folkins. She was convinced I had a book in me on the subject, and, on that note, our working relationship began. Her editorial suggestions were unfailingly tactful and intelligent. Over the months of writing, she was patient and understanding, firm when she needed to be, considerate when she knew I was doing my best to find my way. I've learned a great deal from her about the collaborative process of bringing a manuscript to completion. Senior production editor Sandra Tooze kept *Cool* securely on track in the final stages before publication. Shaun Oakey was copy editor, though the title doesn't do justice to his painstaking work. Shaun challenged my prose, sometimes line by line, inhabiting my sentences to make a better book.

But my thanks go back further still, to colleagues at CBC Radio's program *Ideas:* executive producer Bernie

ACKNOWLEDGMENTS

Lucht and producers Sara Wolch and Max Allen. Their loyalty has been invaluable over the years. Whenever Max came across articles on ice cream, he passed them on to me. He also guided me through the complicated science of making ice cream. The result appears in chapter 3—not in Max's spare, rigorous style, certainly, but bearing his stamp nevertheless. Bernie, Sara, and Max have all been enormously supportive of me and *Cool.* I'm fortunate in my friends.

Michèle Macartney-Filgate made chocolate ice cream for the book, allowing me to stand at her elbow with a microphone and record her every word. It's because of Michèle that I now make my own ice cream, with the electric machine she gave me. And Frances Wainwright knows how much I owe her. Along with Michèle, Frances answered many a worried telephone call, guiding me to safety when the writing wasn't going well. She also shared her memories of ice cream, as did Greg Kelly, Gilbert Reid, May Loo, and others. Collecting those memories was one of the greatest pleasures of this book for me. Raja Alem introduced me to the delights of Middle Eastern *sharab,* or *sharbat,* and gave permission for the publication of her aunt Fatma Hijji's recipe. Erna Paris shared the benefit of her experience as a successful published writer.

Erna knows the ups and downs of the process, and she too was a lifeline. Our friendship goes back to college days. As for Michael Spivak, whom I also met when we were young at the University of Toronto, he's been both cheerleader and mentor over the years, demanding yet just, never letting me get away with anything less than the best I can do. Michael photographed one of the illustrations in *Cool.*

The families of James Logue and Stan Seydegart, who died during the writing of this book, agreed that their contributions should remain part of it. Paul Dickson, author of *The Great American Ice Cream Book,* responded instantly to all my emails; he and his work have been a wonderful source of information. Bill Whitehead gave permission for the use of the snow-bread recipe from Timothy Findley's memoir *From Stone Orchard.* Artist David Gilhooly agreed to the inclusion of a photograph of one of his ceramic pieces that I own. And Roderick Whitfield, professor emeritus of the University of London (Chinese and East Asian art) allowed his translation of the poem by the Sung Dynasty poet Yang Wanli to appear.

The following websites and institutions gave permission to reprint material: allrecipes.com for the *kulfi* recipe; the

CREDITS

ILLUSTRATIONS

LITERARY SOURCES

INDEX

INDEX